Here's a gift for you.
In under 3 minutes, you'll discover...

- How to travel solo in a heartbeat

- The #1 thing that is causing you to lose sleep!

- The secret to becoming a more content and confident woman

  And much, MUCH More...

Download COMPLIMENTARY guide at:

http://www.gutsyladytravel.com/report

Testimonials

"Yes! Yes! Yes! Melanie Eng is a woman after my own heart, a traveller both to the inner and outer reaches. So glad I got the chance to preview this book that is guaranteed to take readers on a joy ride of bravery, meaning, and big fun."

Pam Grout
#1 New York Times bestselling author of 17 books including
*E-Squared: 9 Do-it-Yourself Energy Experiments
to Prove your Thoughts Create your Reality*

"Travelling solo offers women opportunities for growth in ways that can only be understood if you actually go. Grab inspiration from Melanie and *Gutsy Lady Travel*, go solo and forge your own legacy of travel stories and personal strength."

Janice Waugh
Author of *The Solo Traveler's Handbook*
Publisher of Solo Traveler, the blog for those who travel alone

"Melanie Eng relates her unique and special journeys as she shares the joy of travelling solo. Travelling through the pages of this book feels like a journey inward as we follow Melanie's journey. We can embrace who we are, grab our courage and get ready to book our first trip with her and have the time of our life."

Victoria Hargis
Transition Coach
Live Abundantly Through Loss
http://www.victoriahargis.com

"I'm too old to travel alone! It's not safe for a woman to travel alone! Melanie's story will brush those excuses to the side and you will be inspired to jump head first into the "pool" that is your dream trip. Afraid? Don't be! Melanie will jump right in there with you and have you "swimming" on your own in no time! This book will inspire and delight all who read it!"

Deb Amia aka Grammar Queen
www.grammarqueen.com

"Gutsy Lady Travel is a gem. Travelling fuels our life experience and Melanie nailed it. Virtually travelling with her as she jets across the globe was a rare combination of entertainment and education. Get this book."

Jody Temple White
www.TheCourageVibe.com

Printed in Canada

ISBN 13: 978-1530140336

For information regarding the author and the author's services, please contact:

info@gutsyladytravel.com or +1 604 222 7811

"The world is a book, and those who do not travel read only a page."

– Saint Augustine

Dedication

This book is dedicated to Mui, my gutsy and courageous mother who immigrated to Victoria, BC Canada from Guangdong, China to wed my father in an arranged marriage. Also to all the other gutsy and courageous women who travelled on their own.

Acknowledgements

I am grateful for the assistance given by Doug Crowe, my book mentor, for his valuable and constructive suggestions. I appreciate your willingness to give me encouragement and support.

I wish to give my special heartfelt appreciation to Dov and Renuka Baron who assisted and guided me in my personal journey. I am grateful to you both for inspiring me to stand in my power and not give up on myself. Much of what I wrote in this book is my self-discovery about who I was and who I have become: a courageous, empowered woman and an authentic leader.

Thank you, Deb Amia for your eagle-eyed attention to detail. You have gone above and beyond reviewing word by word, line by line, and at the same time focusing on the big picture.

Special thanks to my dear friend, Claudette Bouchard, for your inspiration and encouragement. I treasure our friendship. Thanks for being my cheerleader.

I am deeply grateful to Allan, Alvin, and Andre, my brothers for their trust, love, and confidence in me.

Thank you to my family and friends for their support and encouragement to tell my story.

Preface

Remember when you were in high school? Maybe you would spend the night at your best friend's house? Perhaps, like some, you would talk late into the evening about your dreams and hopes for the future, ranging from marrying the school hunk to landing the dream job and having a perfect house with three well-behaved children.

Embarking on adventures around the world may have also come up, and you both fantasized about sipping cocktails on a sun-drenched beach with glistening, white sand.

Oh, to be young, free, and up for a lifetime full of adventures.

Several decades passed, and some of those things you and your best friend dreamed of came to fruition. Some didn't. And some of the things you yearned for as a teen simply changed.

In the end, for whatever reason, you have ended up single while some of your friends married and had children. With no one to be accountable to, you're free to explore the sights of the world – and truly live every moment to the fullest, embracing different cultures, learning different languages, and sampling local delicacies.

Lately, you've been thinking that that is what you should do – take a chance and explore the wonders of this glorious world in which we live.

But if you've never travelled alone, there is a certain amount of fear, trepidation, and that little voice in your head that says, *"It is not safe for older, single women to travel on their own."*

Should you succumb to this uneasiness of embarking on an adventure alone?

You could sit safely in the comfort of your own home and watch travel shows and documentaries, but it's not the same thing. You won't get the real-life experience of feeling what it's like to have snow fall on your face in New York, or the sun touch your skin in the Caribbean.

A word of caution, *"Wherever You Go, There You Are." –* Jon Kabat-Zinn.

Travelling, however, doesn't mean that you escape from yourself – no matter where you go, what clothes you wear, or what name you use, you are *'you'*, wherever you are. But travelling opens you up to new experiences, and it changes your perspective on life.

This isn't some new age mumbo jumbo. It is one of many simple truths. No matter how near or far you have the courage to go, and no matter how you change your external environment, your internal environment, comprised of your thoughts and beliefs, goes with you.

This simple truth is something Melanie Eng knows oh so very well. How do I know? I know because over the last decade I've seen Melanie take courageous leaps to overcome the restrictions and limitations of her own unexamined beliefs, which had held her back from playing full out, sometimes from even participating.

Today, Melanie has 10 years of not just learning how to break out of those limitations, but of creating a new internal environment with her commitment to integrate small steps every day and play full out.

When I first met Mel she was already an accomplished professional, working with bold-faced names, but she knew there was more to life. So she began exploring within, and discovering the thinking that became her beliefs and controlled her behavior. With guidance, Mel learned, and did what she needed to do to fulfill the dreams she imagined for herself.

While she was on this internal journey, Mel bought and ran a successful business in one of the most beautiful places in British Columbia. Somehow, even though she was running a business that was open seven days a week, she found the time and energy to take the Authentic Speaker Academy for Leadership training (a six-month intensive program) and take her life several levels higher, internally and externally.

Another simple truth I know is that Melanie Eng knows how to serve. She knows first-hand what it's like to be a mature woman travelling solo outside of North America, where codes of conduct may vary for men, but are drastically different for women.

Melanie also knows the value of money, and how hard people work to fulfill their dreams of travelling the world. She ensures that people get more value for every dollar, because that is exactly what they deserve. They deserve only the best!

The biggest simple truth Melanie knows is how fear can prevent you from stepping out of your comfortable and "safe" environment to experience other people, cultures, food, countries, and ultimately, joy.

If you've ever thought about exploring another country, but you haven't done it because you are uncomfortable and afraid to go, let Melanie serve you. She will take the time to get to know who you are, what you enjoy, and what you want to experience. She will design the most enriching and memorable travels to whatever destinations your heart longs for. Because she is well-travelled, externally and internally, she can help you deal with many of the reasons you shied away from getting a passport, packing your bags, and hopping on the plane.

There really are only two choices in life: to play it safe and be gripped by fear, or to really live each moment like it's your last because life, after all, is very precious.

Renuka Baron
Facilitating Courageous Conversations
Women's Empowerment Mentor
Corporate Consultant for Authentic Paragon Alliance Inc.

GUTSY LADY TRAVEL

… How to Build *Unshakeable* Confidence by Travelling

by Melanie Eng

Table of Contents

Introduction

Her toes curled under as she fidgeted in her chair and watched her schoolmates. Each time one was done sharing, the others, who hadn't gone yet, bounced up and down, their arms raised high in the air – hoping to be the next one chosen.

The little girl tried to make herself even smaller, picking at a hangnail, and then sucking her finger as a tiny drop of blood appeared on the edge of her nail.

"Please don't pick me," she silently pleaded with her teacher, glancing up, then swiftly lowering her eyes as she caught the teacher looking at her. She briefly shook her head "no", hoping to convey that the front of the classroom was the last place she wanted to be. "No ... I ... can't ... do ... it.   No ... no." She breathed a sigh of relief as Miss McClung chose Stuart, who sprang out of his chair, ready to show off his brand new toy.

Stuart was large for his age, and well-fed. His metal G.I. Joe lunchbox was often stuffed full with two peanut butter and grape jelly sandwiches, a bag of barbecue potato chips, and a package of Wagon Wheels.

But even as she took a breath, she felt her head recoil when Stuart's elbow struck the back of her head as he walked to the front of the room. Many in the class giggled as the little girl's head shook from the force of the elbow and tears gathered in her eyes. "Stuart, what do we say when we accidentally hurt someone?" asked Miss McClung, bringing the attention of the entire class to the little girl who simply lowered her chin down into her chest, shiny straight black hair swinging forward to shield her face.

"Sorry ... little Chink." Stuart said the first word very loud, and barely whispered the last two as he sneered back at the little girl.

Stuart, finally at the front of the class, held up his new six-inch plastic Godzilla and explained how he and his friends would build cities out of blocks, and then his toy would wipe out all the "Chinks" who lived there.

The little girl slid further down in her chair as once again she felt eyes staring at her, drilling into her back. Even as Stuart once again uttered the word, the little girl wasn't quite sure what he was saying or what it meant, although he'd been calling her that since he caught sight of her on the first day of school. As it turned out, "Chink" is slang for a Chinese person.

"All right, Stuart," said Miss McClung, "there will be none of that in my classroom. See me after school. You may return to your seat." As Stuart started to walk back down the aisle toward her, the little girl braced herself – and was relieved as she heard the teacher said, "No, Stuart, go around this way," and pointed to a route that wouldn't put the little girl in Stuart's pathway.

Her relief was short-lived as she heard her name being called. "Melanie? It's your turn. Come show us what you have brought for show and tell." She felt her face start to heat up as she looked up and shook her head. "No."

"Please, no," silently begging her teacher to understand. "No." But Miss McClung continued to call her. "Melanie, it's your turn. Come up here please."

The little girl finally realized that there was no other choice. She had to obey her teacher. The sound of Miss McClung's stern voice and her eyes peering through her cool cat eye glasses meant she was serious. She slowly rose, shaking, as she felt the heat leave her face, and started to shiver despite the warm, bulky, lime green sweater she was wearing. She shuffled slowly to the front of the room, wondering if, perhaps, she could make a dash out the door to run away and hide forever. Her shoulders hunched as she reached the front of the class. She glanced up to see that all eyes were glued on her empty hands.

She had nothing to share. No pretty plastic tea set – the perfect size for a tea party with friends (if only she had at least one friend). She had no bright pink yo-yo to play tricks with as the plastic bobbed up and down. She hadn't brought anything to school for 'Show and Tell'. She had no toys, no books, nothing to offer. So she just stood there. Silent. Frightened.

Miss McClung smiled down and placed her hand gently on the little girl's shoulder. "As most of you know, Melanie is very quiet, but today she wanted to show you something that she has that no one else in the whole world has. As you know, there are many, many Barbie dolls, and many tiddlywinks, and …,"she glanced at Stuart, "many, many Godzilla monsters, but today, Melanie wanted to show you her beautiful, lime green sweater."

"Melanie, you're wearing such a stunning sweater. It's so soft and warm … and look at the two cute kittens on the front." Melanie began to get hotter as she felt beads of sweat on her forehead and felt her back dampen. She dreaded being the centre of attention.

"As you can all see, there is also another big, black kitten playing with a ball of yarn on the back of her sweater." Miss McClung twirled Melanie around.

"Isn't this beautiful?" She looked at the class, nodding her head up and down as most of the girls, and a few of the boys, did the same. Miss McClung smiled as she felt Melanie stand up a bit straighter.

"Boys and girls," she addressed the class, "do you know what knitting is?" She glanced around. "Stuart, do you know what knitting is?" He didn't answer. "Does anyone here know how you start to knit?" She had the full attention of the entire class.

"Well, you start with a piece of string called yarn, and you have two long sticks with a point on the end." She smiled as she talked. "They're called knitting needles. And as you wrap the yarn around the needles in a certain way, it starts to create a sweater like this ... only rarely as pretty as this. So Melanie is the only person in the whole wide world who has a sweater like this. What a lucky girl you are, Melanie." She gave Melanie's shoulder beneath her hand a small squeeze. "OK, Melanie. You may go sit down now."

As she returned to her desk, the little girl still knew that the rest of the class was staring at her, only this time it wasn't as openly hostile, and some of the girls were actually smiling at her – somewhat of a first.

After that day, things changed for Melanie, and the little girls that used to pick on her and ignore her actually became her friends. They would spend their recesses teaching her how to speak perfect English.

That shy little girl was me.

I was not only the shy, awkward girl who was different than the rest of the kids in school, I looked different too. I was the one with slanted black eyes, straight black hair in a ponytail, who didn't know any words in English before I started school.

Gutsy Lady Travel is a journey that has not ended for me, yet.
But this is where it began ...

Chapter One

East Meets West Childhood

" *There is always one moment in childhood when the door opens and lets the future in.* "

– Graham Greene

My childhood was a dance between two cultures. While at home, we lived a stark existence. Although my paternal grandmother was born in Victoria, BC, Canada, making me third generation Canadian, in reality I lived in a traditional Chinese household. My dad spent long hours away from home working in the rice paddy fields of Victoria, BC growing carrots, lettuce, green onions, and purple beets that he sold to the local supermarkets. Although he spoke perfect English, around home he mainly conversed in Cantonese because my mother didn't speak English. So, until I started school, I only spoke Cantonese. I didn't attend pre-school and I never had any social interactions with other children that allowed any preparation for my first day at school and what I was about to endure.

It wasn't until the first grade that I was thrust into a completely different universe – an alien world where I watched from the sidelines as my schoolmates laughed, shouted, ran, and played, often paying little or no attention to the little Asian girl who stood silently, too scared to join in and unable to communicate in any way.

It was a very lonely existence.

I was gripped by fear – paralyzed by it, in fact. I feared I wouldn't fit in and therefore I didn't. My fellow students soon discovered I was an easy target and taunted me.

"Little Chink." I kept hearing that word. Mostly it was the boys who said it to me, but I didn't know what it meant. I was quite sure, however, that it wasn't a very nice word. "Chink." I rolled the word around in my mouth, trying to taste it, trying to pronounce it. "Cheeeenk." The sound went around and around in my head. I recalled both the sound and the look on the face of the bully as he gave me a shove and spit the word at me. "Watch it, CHINK!" he tormented, as he and his friends walked away snickering, his friends slapping him on the back in a celebratory way.

Standing alone on the asphalt of the school playground, wrapping my arms around each other as I fingered the soft woolen yarn of my sweater, I tried to make sense from something that clearly made none. I was completely different from all the other students with their wide eyes and fair skin – the girls with their curled hair, pink ribbons, and store-bought, pretty, coloured dresses. I glanced around and once again pulled on the homemade kitten sweater my aunt had so lovingly knit.

"Hi," a soft voice from behind me said. "Don't let them bother you. They're just boys with cooties."

"Yeah," another welcoming voice chimed in. "They're mad because girls rule, boys drool."

Still not knowing what they said, I watched as several girls from my classroom surrounded me and giggled at what she'd announced. But for the first time since I'd entered this strange new place called "school", I realized that they weren't laughing at me. It was such a relief, I actually smiled.

"Say something in Chinese," a redheaded girl with copper freckles splattered across her nose requested.

"Yeah ... we want to hear you talk in Chinese," the one with brunette pigtails who'd first greeted me, asked. It turned out her name was Katherine, and she seemed to be the leader of the girls. I'd noticed her in class, constantly raising her hand to be called upon. She was also the one Miss McClung scolded and told to stop talking. She spoke quickly, with a rapid staccato punctuating each sentence.

I kept quiet.

"Maybe she doesn't understand what we're saying." They all looked at me, wide-eyed.

Sue, the redheaded girl, leaned forward and yelled, "SAY SOMETHING IN CHINESE!!!" Everyone, including me, jumped.

"Why did you yell like that?" asked Debbie, the one wearing a plaid dress who had a short, blond, pixie haircut.

"SO SHE CAN HEAR ME!"

"She can hear you, silly ... she just doesn't understand," explained Valerie, a quiet girl who rarely spoke. "She doesn't know our words, but I like her. I think she's nice. And I LOOOOVE kittens." She reached out to stroke the kittens on my sweater.

She looked intently at me. I lowered my eyes, afraid of further attention, but still felt her look burrowing into my face.

"Do you want to be my friend?" I didn't understand what she was saying, but she looked friendly.

"I'm Katherine." She pointed at herself. "Katherine" she repeated.

Then she pointed at my chest and said my name. "Melanie. You're Melanie."

She pointed back at herself. "Katherine." Then she pointed back at me. "Melanie." Repeating this several times, she then proceeded to point to the rest of the smiling girls. "Sue. Debbie. Barbara. Valerie." She paused, then pointed back to me. "Melanie." I nodded slightly, indicating that I understood.

"Melanie." I said, and then looked at her. "Kath … Kath …."

"KATHERINE," the group said in unison. I nodded. "Katherine."

And so it began. I had finally found friends – friends who were kind enough to teach me English – and they were just six-year-old school-mates.

My journey into a brave, new world had begun. Even though I was still very shy, I was very much aware of the differences between my life and theirs. Their kindness is something that will always be with me. It set me on a course to create the life that I have today; that is something that I am eternally grateful for.

What about you? What distant childhood memory gives you a warm feeling?

www.gutsyladytravel.com/www.gutsyladytravel.ca

Chapter Two

Experience Your Life As Though It Were Chocolate

"The greatest thing in this world is not so much where we stand as in what direction we are moving."

– Johann Wolfgang von Goethe

What is your journey? We all have different paths, different journeys, and even contrasting goals and ways to achieve them. My journey isn't like yours. I grew up in a family that was poor and, until we had our vegetable stand, we were unable to really even afford the basics in life. It was just plain white rice and vegetables, and occasionally, a piece of candy.

Candy is always sweet and satisfying. Can someone live on candy? Of course not but, eaten in moderation, candy can be one of the absolute joys in life. That first whiff of a chocolate bar, biting into the strong burst of a lemon jawbreaker, the mass of fluffy, spun, pink cotton candy from the local fair, all of these are delicious drops of sweetness.

In my candy-loving opinion, Forrest Gump's mother had it right.

"Life IS like a box of chocolates. You never know what you're going to get." My box of chocolates is travel – the pleasure of planning my trips. What unique place should I visit next? What time of year? How long will the adventure be this time? What to do? What food to indulge in? So many exciting decisions to make – and quite honestly, from that first sweet, sticky bite of planning my trip, until the last lick of my fingers as I return, I enjoy it all. Oh, of course there can be parts of the trip that are frustrating, scary, or give you a tummy ache. When you bite into that box of chocolates, you never know what you're going to get.

I meet people, especially women, who are leading lives of quiet desperation. Often, they're women in my generation who grew up believing that we didn't deserve the candy of life. Sometimes it's cultural, but often it's just conditioning. We're raised to think that, instead of opening that box of chocolates, we should crawl inside the box and carefully avoid even nibbling on the chocolate. So often, so many of us have the mindset that we shouldn't enjoy the chocolate. We're so caught up in life – and making everyone else happy – that we forget to experience the joy of life itself.

Single or married, most women have been conditioned to think of others first. Perhaps it is our nurturing instinct, but it doesn't matter. If it isn't a husband or kids, it can just as easily be a parent or two, a boss, or a job. What about you? Perhaps you're married with children who are almost grown. How can you forget the early mornings where you were the first one in the household awake? Your feet hit the floor first and you were immediately involved in letting the dog out to do his thing. Then getting breakfast on the table for the kids. Perhaps they're picky, so you cater to a different choice for each kid and your husband. Meanwhile, you're standing over the sink, barely able to grab a bit of dry toast and slurp rapidly cooling coffee. You're also yelling at the kids to get out of bed and hoping against hope that they make that bed as they stumble in half asleep to take a couple of bites of breakfast. Then it's getting dressed, grabbing homework, checking do they have this, don't forget that. Oh, and soccer practice, or ballet practice, or Boy or Girl Scouts after school. If you're a working mother, you're also trying to get yourself dressed, hair done, makeup on, and get off so you're not late for work. And so it goes, year after year. Occasionally, you may have gazed longingly at an exotic picture of a Caribbean cruise, thinking how lovely it would be to just sail off, leaving everything behind. But then a phone call from the principal at your son's school (letting you know that he threw a spit wad at the little girl he has a crush on), brings reality crashing down upon your head.

Or maybe you've devoted a large portion of your life to being a career woman. You've given up the dream of a family in order to climb that corporate ladder, in the hopes of breaking through that dreaded glass ceiling. When others were taking off on two-week vacations to Hawaii, you peeked out the window and wondered how to squeeze in the time between deadlines at work and bringing your elderly parent to the doctor's office. The life you've experienced is an 80-hour work week and a closet full of Ann Taylor suits.

Now, let's fast forward 15 or 20 years. Inside, you still feel 23 and yet, who is that middle-aged (a tad frumpy), slightly gray-haired lady in the mirror? The view is kind of fuzzy and you lower the glasses you've pushed up in order to get a good look at the extra 20 lbs. and sagging breasts that are staring back at you. Oh, my God! I've turned into my MOTHER!!!

Where DID those 30 years go? Maybe the time passed by, taking with it the thrill of first love, the heartbeats of your first child, or the gut-wrenching agony of going to the funeral of your best friend. Perhaps there are scars from cancer surgery, or internal scars, barely healed from a divorce.

What about your house? Is it quiet compared to all those years ago when kids were running around the back yard, yelling and throwing water balloons, the dog was barking and the TV was blaring? Do you miss it?

What about the years of taking care of everyone else? Remember the hours of making sure the kids were safe? Did you invest your heart and soul into ensuring your partner's health was up to snuff? Or perhaps you were given the responsibility of being the primary caregiver for your elderly mother with dementia?

So now, isn't it time? Isn't it time for you to start enjoying yourself, your life? You deserve to start living – to squeeze every drop from life that you possibly can. You deserve to experience that box of chocolates, to take a bite and discover the pleasant surprise inside.

Oh, what would happen if you if you were to open up that box, lean over, and take a whiff of the deep, rich chocolate candies in that box? Would you inevitably start craving just one tiny, little lick? Just a meagre taste? And, oh my, what about just grabbing a piece and shoving it into your mouth? As you bite down, you discover the surprise in the centre. Maybe the centre is filled with cherry that oozes out that red syrup. Or perhaps caramel topped with sea salt that marry together so perfectly. Once in a while, it might be a chocolate that's rare and surprising. I once took a bite of a dark chocolate and lavender flavored piece of chocolate. It was unique and remarkable and delicious.

And that is what embarking on world adventures is like.

I have met so many women who took a chance and travelled the world by themselves, and throughout this book, I'll share some of their enlightening stories that will also inspire you to take a chance and REALLY embrace life.

An Encounter with a Real Life Prince

> **" A good traveler has no fixed plans and is not intent on arriving. "**

— Lao Tzu

One of my friends I met during my travels, LOVED to travel and had many fascinating stories to tell.

I was sitting at Starbucks in Covent Garden in London on a rainy Tuesday when Jane asked to borrow my cell phone charger. We struck up a conversation and she recounted how she had just come back from a month-long trip to India.

Her story involved an encounter with two famous celebrities, the couple's countless security, and a real life Indian prince.

Jane was an Australian journalist who had a thirst for life and adventure. She had decided, on a whim, to take a trip to India. As she tells it, she arrived in Mumbai after a long haul flight on Air India and stumbled out of the airport to the screams of Indian men trying to coach her into their cabs. She stood out like a sore thumb, given she was 5'9" and blond – in fact, she towered over most Indian men.

Jane had no idea where she was headed or where she was going to stay, so she decided to jump into a cab with a driver who could speak some English, and off to the Grand Hyatt Mumbai she went.

She was shaken when, upon her arrival at the gates to the hotel, two burly security guards carrying machetes pounded on the window and demanded that the trunk of the cab be opened. As it turned out, this was standard practice because the hotels were checking for weapons.

Back in November 2008, *The New York Times* reported that coordinated terrorist attacks struck the heart of Mumbai, killing dozens in machine gun and grenade assaults on at least two five-star hotels, the city's largest train station, a Jewish centre, a movie theatre, and a hospital.

The city had been reeling ever since those fatal attacks and was somewhat living on edge.

But back to Jane's story. She finally arrived at the front desk, and thankfully, they had rooms available. As her luck would have it, there was a room available on the VIP floor. She booked it for several days, checked in, and ordered a bottle of red Shiraz wine.

She was exhausted.

Around five a.m., a banging on the door woke Jane – she was petrified.

She went to the door, looked out the peephole, and saw a brawny, bald man. He looked menacing. With trepidation, she opened the door, leaving the chain on.

"I know who you are," the man said in a British accent.

"You do?" she said, meekly.

"I'll be keeping an eye on you," he said, earnestly, and walked away.

She closed the door. She knew she had seen him somewhere before. Then it dawned on her, he is the bodyguard for a famous celebrity couple. How did he know who she was? When checking into the hotel, the front desk took a copy of her passport and visa. Her visa stated that she was a journalist.

Shaken, she tried to go back to sleep, but she couldn't.

She got up, showered, and headed downstairs for the breakfast buffet. The burly bodyguard was nowhere to be seen. Instead, seated at a table across from her, were four other equally menacing men — they gave her the evil eye. Shaking, she grabbed her food and decided it was better to eat in her room than sit and be given death stares.

Still plagued with jet lag and a night with no sleep, she passed out just after breakfast.

Waking up around four p.m., Jane showered, and decided to go to the hotel bar's happy hour.

She sat down at the bar and a mid-age British man next to her turned to her and asked her where she was from.

"Australia," she said, "but I live in London now."

"I just moved from London to here," the man said. "I'm Jeff," he said, extending his hand out to her.

Jeff was one of a large number of British people who had flooded Mumbai to work in the tech business. The money was good, the cost of living low, and it meant they could save money and eventually go home and live a comfortable life – far from the strains that governed life in England with the working class.

They chatted for an hour over two glasses of wine and then decided to venture out of the confinements of the hotel and discover Mumbai's nightlife.

Several bars and several drinks later, they found a Mumbai "hot spot" (a nightclub packed with wealthy Indians where Western music blared from the speakers).

Jeff and Jane decided a shot was in order as they took in the sights before them.

A handsome man made his way to the bar and headed directly to Jane.

"Hi," he said.

A little perplexed, but flattered, she said, "Hi."

From there the two embarked on an hour-long conversation. Later, he offered Jane and Jeff a ride back to the hotel in his black BMW, where the three of them had another drink.

It turned out "Mr. Charisma" was a real life prince and for the four re-maining days, Jane had her own princely tour guide. Jeff became quite busy with work, thus Jane and "the prince" toured the area, laughed until they cried, and began a whirlwind romance that ended as quickly as it had begun.

As Jane described it, it was not exactly a Cinderella story, but based on reality. As culture gaps are sometimes insurmountable, a relationship would not be in the cards.

Some people are in our lives for a season, a reason, or forever. Most of the time, it's the first two. When travelling … embrace the reality.

www.gutsyladytravel.com/www.gutsyladytravel.ca

Chapter Three

Travelling Out of Our Comfort Zone

" We travel, some of us forever, to seek other places, other lives, other souls. "

– Anais Nin

What is it like to travel internationally … alone? For some, it's a way of life. For others, it's a 'once in a lifetime' event. For me, it started as an escape from the stresses of home life. To me, travelling was freedom; a freedom that I craved.   I was like a junkie feeling the euphoric rush of travelling and cramming as many experiences as possible into each and every journey.

Travelling also opens up the possibility of crossing paths with people you ordinarily wouldn't meet in your day-to-day life, like Jane's example of the Indian prince.

Yes, I admit I was terrified of the unknown. What would happen if I were trapped in a foreign country, unable to free myself? Both fear and excitement release the same adrenalin, the difference is in how our brains interpret that feeling. So, while I often have to admit that I was afraid, I was also excited to get out and see the rest of the world. The freedom, sense of adventure, and just plain fun that I experience has driven me to travel to over 40 different countries so far. It was this spirit that allowed me to meet Mohammed when I was in Egypt.

I looked outside of the airplane's window onto a vast openness of beige-coloured sand everywhere, except for a huge patch of green, which was a golf course. I thought, *'It's a shame to waste so much water to keep it green and lush looking.'* There was a young man in his late 20s sitting beside me.

"Where are you from?"

"Canada," I replied, as I turned my back quickly to look out the window. I was in no mood to talk to a stranger, especially a man. Actually, my mind was focused on going home and sleeping in my own comfy bed again. His dark, piercing eyes made me feel nervous, but I could not know that this trip was about to become a blessing in disguise.

"My name is Mohammed. What is your name?" he asked.

"Melanie," I answered, abruptly.

"I am going home to Alexandria for a few days. Have you been to Alexandria yet?"

"No."

"Do you want to visit Alexandria?"

"No, thanks. I am going home soon." By now, I was frustrated with his endless questions.

"When are you going home?"

"Soon." I was being vague.

"You can visit me in Alexandria and stay at my place."

I gave him the look of *'Are you out of your bloody mind?'*

"Look, I don't want to harm you, I don't want money from you," he said, staring into my terrified eyes.

In shock and lost for words, I wondered 'What the hell does he want?' I was face-to-face with an Egyptian man. My body was experiencing a 'fight-or-flight' response. My clammy, sweaty back was pressed against the window, and my heart was thumping. I was cornered and I couldn't escape.

"I just want to show you my hometown, Alexandria," he said.

Fighting back tears of relief, I sat back down in my seat.

"You have to see Alexandria. It is much different than Cairo. You have time to visit Alexandria? There is a train that leaves Cairo. You can take the nine a.m. train tomorrow. I will meet you at the train station. Here's my cell number. Call me tonight if you want to go," he said.

I was scared and unsure, and too shy and cautious to disclose personal information. I was also, of course, baffled and suspicious of his offer.

"Let me think about it. I will call you if I decide to do it."

"You do have time to visit, and you can even stay overnight if you like." My mind was full of 'what if' scenarios: 'What if I am kidnapped? What if I don't make it home? What if I become a sex slave?'

We were both flying from Sharm el-Sheikh, a resort along the Red Sea, to Cairo.

Mohammed had a couple of days off from his job as an assistant manager at one of the deluxe hotels in Sharm el-Sheikh. His English was good. Throughout the journey, it was his friendly and well-mannered demeanor that put me at ease, and I started to trust him.

I arrived at the hotel around five p.m., still holding onto the little piece of paper with Mohammed's name and number on it. I was torn between wanting to see Alexandria with Mohammed and remembering that I was

19

a single woman all alone in Egypt. Part of my mind screamed '*Code Orange, High Alert: Don't go! Stay! You will get hurt!*' and the other part perceived his gesture as innocent. You know how a stranger's actions or words can instill fear in another person? Even the smallest movement or the way certain words are conveyed can trigger fear in one person, but not in another. It's all due to our individual conditioning.

Yet, my heart wanted to see another part of Egypt. I hadn't been to Alexandria before and my heart spoke to me: '*Go! Trust!*'

My hand was shaking as I started to dial Mohammed's phone number, then I suddenly hung up like a nervous teenager calling a boy for the first time. I had a brief moment of terror. I composed myself and dialed the number again, very slowly.

Just as I was about to hang up, I heard "Hello."

"Hi, Mohammed, this is Melanie."

"Hi, Melanie! Are you coming to Alexandria tomorrow?"

"Yes, I will be on the nine a.m. train tomorrow," I replied.

"Nine o'clock will be great. See you tomorrow at the train station," Mohammed exclaimed. He sounded enthusiastic.

As I hung up the phone, I felt like there was a roller coaster in my stomach. There was an array of emotions — elation, exhilaration, fear, and terror. I could not believe I decided to meet a complete stranger for a day tour. I felt shock, but also there was a spark of excitement. My courageous and adventurous side arose and awoke my desire to have fun — an aspect of myself that had lain dormant for decades. It seemed it was ready to be unearthed again.

I treasured the "wild" and brave childhood times I spent with my brothers, doing things for the pure enjoyment of fun, without our parents' knowledge. The last time I really let loose was when I was 12. I and my two younger brothers, aged 11 and 8, wanted to be the first Marco Polos to discover the 'secret cave' on Mount Douglas. We were ready to fight off any wild lions to become famous household names at school. But we didn't fight off any wild beasts, and we barely made it to the mountain's base before we turned back. We didn't care. What mattered was that we had fun and had the freedom to wander. We had connected and bonded with one another, and those memories could never be taken away. When I finally located the 'secret cave' years later, it was no bigger than a dog house.

Just thinking about our search for the cave made me realize that going to meet Mohammed was something that I wanted to do. My thoughts about my childhood days of adventure inspired me to have fun by taking a train to Alexandria to meet him for the day. And I was even more enthusiastic knowing a local was willing to show me his hometown.

Shortly after I called Mohammed, I sprang into action. How was I going to get to the train station? I quickly put on my shoes and headed downstairs to the hotel lobby.

"Good evening. I'm going to Alexandria tomorrow morning. Can you please tell me where the train station is?" I asked the hotel manager. He was friendly, neatly dressed in a gray business suit, and eager to assist me.

"Yes, madam," he surprised me by answering in an upper crust, British accent. Then he turned and called out in Arabic to an elderly man who appeared from the back room.

"No, it is ok … I only need you to write down the instructions for me. I don't want to impose on the gentleman," I said.

"No! No! I insist. This man will take you there right now." Another flash of fear almost overtook me; however, I swallowed my fear and accepted his offer.

That evening, he took me on a practice run so I would know the route the next morning. We walked slowly through the darkness to the train station and he took my left hand as he led the way. The softness of the elderly man's hand in mine felt secure and safe, like a father holding his child's hand. He had a gentle soul, a toothless smile, and deep wrinkles on his face. He was dressed in a traditional long, gray shirt called a "gallabiyah" with a kaftan on top, which was bound with a woven belt. His head was wrapped in a white turban.

It was a cool winter evening as we slowly made our way along the sidewalk. It was a 15 minute walk to the Ramses train station.

We strolled slowly in the darkness of the road. It was the very first time I had walked in the dark in Cairo. I was feeling a bit nervous as I peered over my shoulder every few steps. The street was quiet; the leaves of the palm tree gently swayed in the breeze. We finally arrived at Ramses Station. It was an old concrete building, which was refurbished in 1955. We were barely through the entranceway when I saw a big sign in English – "Alexandria." There wasn't a soul in sight and it was dark and peaceful.

The old man smiled and pointed at the sign. I nodded and returned his smile.

As we returned to the hotel, I practiced the little Arabic that I had learned. "Thank you" I said in Arabic as I slipped an Egyptian dollar into his soft hand. He revealed a big, toothless smile as I looked into his innocent eyes.

"Thank you for having the gentleman show me the way to the train station," I told the hotel manager.

"My pleasure, madam. I suggest you purchase a first class ticket for your train ride. Good night."

"Shukran. Good night," I said, as I made my way back to my room.

I did it! I took that next brave step toward freeing my soul. I was so elated that I forgot to barricade the room with my suitcase and hotel chair. I was no longer a prisoner in my room.

I started preparing for my trip. I laid out my clothes for the next day.

I wasn't able to sleep through the night as a result of my excitement. I kept turning over and checking the time so I wouldn't oversleep. I woke up just before six a.m. to prepare for my two-and-a-half hour train ride to Alexandria. I quickly brushed my teeth and got dressed in my beige-coloured long pants and white, cotton top. I wanted to respect their custom by covering my arms and legs in case I was going to enter into a mosque. I stuffed my camera, bottled water, some Egyptian pounds, a bag of trail mix, and sunscreen in my red backpack. The weight of the backpack was pretty hefty. 'Ms. Marco (Melanie) Polo' was on another adventurous journey.

I left my passport in the hotel safety deposit box along with my valuables. I had no map and no mobile device. In my excitement, I even forgot to bring photo identification.

It's one of the most courageous decisions of my life. I was scared and not sure if I should leave a note regarding my whereabouts. The hotel didn't even have internet connection.

You know how we do certain things that we're afraid to tell others about? Perhaps we're scared of their response or we don't want to explain what we are doing? Well, that was my story. I knew my family and friends would probably freak out. They weren't even aware I was travelling alone. When I left, everyone, including me, was under the impression that I was joining a tour group of travellers from across North America; however, that wasn't the case. I didn't want to be bombarded with negativity if I told them I ended up on a "Tour de Uno."

At the last minute, my gut instinct told me to leave a note on the bed nightstand, physical evidence for the CSI (Crime Scene Investigator). My note read, "December 6, 2000. This is Melanie Eng and I have gone to Alexandria for the day with Mohammed. His cell number is XXX-XXXX-XXX. If I do not return, this is his information." In my eagerness, I realized I didn't even know his last name or where he worked. I triple checked to ensure my note was visible on the nightstand.

23

I headed downstairs to the dining area for breakfast. The main dining room was grandiose with huge, sparkly chandeliers and thick, plush, woven carpet with smartly dressed waiters. There was definitely a British flare to the famous place as the Shepheard Hotel implies. There was a hustle and bustle about. Just as I sat down, the waiter with a hint of salt-peppery-coloured hair, placed a white, cotton napkin on my lap.

"Good morning, madam. Coffee or tea?" he asked, in perfect English.

"I would like orange juice, please."

By now I felt comfortable sitting alone eating breakfast without worrying what the other patrons thought of me. I had many occasions during this trip to practice, so it came naturally to me now. It was hard for me to fathom that it was only a week ago that I was more alarmed about eating alone than feeling safe. In the beginning, I ate my two week supply of snacks within two days; I was too scared to venture out for nosh. When I finally had the nerve to dine out, 'McDonald's' restaurant was a quick dining buddy. I knew every single item on the menu board off by heart.

Today, I gave myself sufficient time to enjoy a sit down breakfast as I was celebrating my courage to carry on my solo trip, and it was my 40th birthday.

"Here you are, madam," the young waiter promptly placed a beautifully cooked ham omelet in front of me.

"Shukran," I smiled.

It took me a while to dig in my backpack for the piece of paper with details of Mohammed's cell number and the instructions to Ramses train station - turn right from the main entrance of the hotel and then left and left again.

Now, I do have to admit, at that moment I was still feeling somewhat nervous about whether I had made the right choice. My heart started to race as I stopped at the concierge to tell the manager I was heading to Alexandria by train and to confirm the directions.

It Sounds Like ...

❝Be brave. Take risks. Nothing can substitute experience.❞

– Paulo Coelho

The walk to the Ramses train station was different in the morning; however, the steps were retraceable from the night before. I stopped in front of the same "Alexandria" bold sign. There were only five Egyptians dressed in their traditional attire ahead of me in the ticket lineup.

"One ticket to Alexandria," I requested, holding up one finger.

"One way? What class ticket?" asked the young, male attendant in broken English.

"One way and first class ticket. Shukran."

At the train platform, I was greeted by a sea of gray gallabiyahs and kaftans as the rush hour commuters waited patiently for the train.

There wasn't an orderly lineup to get onto the train – it was every man and woman for himself or herself. The train arrived, and when the doors slid open, everyone slowly inched their way in, including me. It was a very claustrophobic feeling as we were tightly packed like sardines. I felt uncomfortable as various arms, elbows, and handbags poked into my body. It was hot and stuffy. I felt my glasses sliding down my nose. I became more and more nervous, and suddenly started wondering if I'd taken the correct train. I assumed it was the right train because there was a sign for "Alexandria" and the elderly gentleman showed me the previous night. As a precaution, I checked twice to make sure the train was heading to Alexandria.

"Hello. Alexandria?" I asked a seated, 30ish woman wearing dark sunglasses. She ignored me as her eyes steadily gazed into the distance. I glanced around and noticed I was the only foreigner on board. When I carefully turned left, I came cheek to cheek with a gentleman in his late 40s with a dark beard.

"Alexandria?" I asked, nervously. He shook his head "no". Again, I asked and again he shook his head "no".

I immediately panicked. Then the train stopped for more passengers and additional people piled in. I heard the train's door close. It was too late to get off – we were packed in so tightly that I couldn't even make my way to the door. I could feel sweat running down my back and my glasses were beginning to steam up. A minute passed, when I heard the train slowing down.

'Shit! Get off now! This is not the time to be a patient and polite Canadian excusing her way through the crowd of commuters,' I thought. As soon as the train's doors opened, I forced my way out, pushing with both arms and using the weight of my backpack to bulldoze through the crowd. I barely made it out before the doors slid shut.

I stood all alone at the train stop without a person in view. I was on the verge of bursting into tears. There were no exits in sight, so I walked 100 feet to the stairs leading up. I looked at the time and realized that I needed to act fast, otherwise, I would miss my train. I jogged up the stairs huffing and puffing, starting to wonder if this was such a good idea. The early morning warm weather was already wearing me down. At the top of the stairs, I looked around and realized that I was in the part of town with many vegetable stalls. Some Egyptian men were going about their business as they unloaded crates of bright orange carrots from a truck. I didn't see any tourists. I looked at my watch again and it was 8:48 a.m. I started to panic as I had exactly 12 minutes to catch the train to Alexandria.

"Speak English?" I asked several local Egyptian men. They all looked at me briefly and ignored me.

I was lost! I needed to find the correct platform. Like many people, I was rather "directionally dyslexic." It was a challenge for me to figure out directions even if I carried three maps, a compass, and a GPS guidance system. I kept asking people walking by if they spoke English. They all looked at me, clueless. I began to feel more and more frustrated and angry, as I realized that the older men don't speak English. I needed to find a younger male, preferably cute, who was learning English in school. My watch said 8:54. I saw a male teenager! I jumped in joy.

"Speak English?" I asked as I ran up to him.

With a warm smile, he held his index finger and thumb barely touching together. With a slight shrug of his shoulders, he indicated that he spoke very little English.

"Train? Alexandria?" I repeated at least three times. He still didn't understand me.

"Alexandria," I said, pointing to my watch and holding up nine fingers. I tugged my ear saying "It sounds like choo-choo." I gestured like the final seconds of a championship game of charades. Finally, he understood and pointed left saying something in Arabic. I shrugged and gave him a puzzled look like 'I don't understand'.

He motioned me to follow him. By now, it was 8:59 and I grabbed his arm, pointed to my watch, and held up nine fingers. We started running, rounding the corner and heading down a staircase. As we ran toward the platform, he stopped and pointed down, meaning "here" is where you wait. Out of breath and panting, I made it!

"Shukran! Shukran!" I thanked him profusely. Relieved, I was ready to hug him.

He nodded in acknowledgement and grinned as he walked away, shaking his head at the crazy Westerner.

Within seconds, the train arrived. I stepped through the doors and yelled, "Shukran!" and waved good-bye. I made my way to the first class seats where the seats were clean, comfortable, and there was air-conditioning. There were only four other businessmen in the compartment, all on their mobile devices. I chose the window seat to catch a glimpse of what was out there along the Nile River. There were scattered straw, thatched dwellings where the nomad farmers live amongst their farm animals. They were farmers who farm the same area their ancestors did along the fertile land of the Nile River. The vast farmland reminded me of the family farm as a child; the serenity, along with the freedom to wander. I saw gigantic, super-sized heads of cauliflower and huge carrots on a horse-drawn cart when the tourist van passed by. The cauliflowers were at least the size of two human heads. The only difference in the farmland was, there were palm trees in Egypt. I didn't want to miss anything so a nap was out of the question.

I felt safe enough to stretch my legs. Strangely, there were no announcements at each stop. I was only able to gauge it by my watch – get off in approximately two and a half hours.

"Hello. Is this stop Alexandria?" I asked an Egyptian businessman.

He nodded "yes" and rose from his seat. I double-checked my seat, ensuring nothing was left behind. To my relief, Mohammed was there to greet me, standing off to the side of the platform. He was dressed in Western blue jeans and a casual, blue dress shirt.

"How was the ride?"

"Good. There is beautiful scenery from the train. I got on the train heading the wrong way, but with the help of a young teenager, got on the right train."

"Are you ready to see Alexandria?"

"Ready! Let's go," I nodded eagerly.

"I will take you to a museum," he proudly announced.

"I love museums," I said. "I really like the Egyptian Museum of Antiquities in Cairo. I already went, but want to go back again before I return home. I can't believe I saw a sitting, mummified monkey!"

"This museum isn't like the one in Cairo," he said. "It is smaller, but there are many artifacts that are older than what is in the Cairo museum."

En route to the museum, we wove our way through smelly, dirty, and run-down streets. Many buildings were in dire need of a fresh coat of paint and major repairs. He knew the shortcuts. He walked fast as I followed closely on his heels.

We arrived at the white-coloured museum that looked more like a mini colonial house than a museum. He was right. There were hundreds, perhaps thousands, of archaeological pieces in whole pieces and small bits strewn everywhere, inside and outside. They were propped along the stairwell, bunched together on the window sill, and piled high in a disorderly fashion outside in the courtyard. These artifacts were treated like they were ordinary rocks among a pile of stones. It was a hoarder's paradise.

"I can't believe these artifacts are tossed aside everywhere," I said.

"Yes, we are tired of seeing all these rocks (artifacts). There is so much that we have nowhere else to put them. My parents prepaid an apartment that is going to be built soon. The builder started digging up the ground and they found artifacts. They did not want to tell the government because they would stop building and we wouldn't have an apartment, so we didn't tell anyone. We don't want these rocks," he exclaimed in frustration. I was mortified as he heaved a slab across his chest, crushing it into a thousand pieces.

"See! I hate these useless pieces of rock that they keep accumulating. Look! It's everywhere!" he yelled. No one came running out.

It certainly was an eye-opener to hear what the local Egyptians thought about the artifacts. Unfortunately, I wasn't good at asking questions or communicating with others. I was more of a geek, too afraid to ask Mohammed about him and his family.

"I am ready to go now. There sure are a lot of artifacts! Can we go somewhere to get something to drink? I am thirsty," I said. Real food was on my mind rather than quenching my thirst.

"I don't know if there are any places that are open. It is Ramadan. We will go to the club and there will be something to drink there," he answered.

Again, we walked to the club with a shortcut in mind. Mohammed took me to the country club where he was a member in his teens. I was pleasantly surprised. Like other posh country clubs in North America, there was a strict dress code and it was furnished with many amenities, such as swimming pools and tennis courts. The biggest feature was a green and lush golf course.

"Are you sure we are allowed to walk on this golf course?" I asked, nervously, ready to dodge any flying golf balls.

"No one will see us," he replied.

I felt like an underage teenager sneaking past security in order to get access to the clubhouse. We walked past four holes to access the clubhouse. I felt light-headed, as I needed something to eat. It had been at least five hours since breakfast. My bottle of water was now empty and my right heel started to blister from all the walking. I noticed the golf course had many short palm trees full of dates.

"Can you eat these dates? I have never eaten a fresh date before," I questioned.

"Yes," he answered, as he picked a couple off the palm tree and handed me a couple of brown, smooth-skinned dates.

"They are so sweet and tasty," I replied as I popped them in my mouth. My stomach was growling for more.

By now, I felt more comfortable with Mohammed. We slowly started talking about ourselves; we began talking about our families. We both were the oldest children in the family. He had only a younger brother. He disclosed that he is careered-oriented and he doesn't have a girl-friend. I had briefly wondered if he was interested in me and wanting a date out of the day. He was non-traditional and definitely a non-con-formist. I felt safe in his presence, knowing that he just wanted to show me Alexandria and liked meeting foreigners.

As we reached the clubhouse, I noticed a group of handsome, athletic, male tennis players smartly dressed in white, sitting at a round table con-versing in Arabic as they laughed and drank cold beverages. I bought a pack of cookies, a soda drink, and a bottle of water. Mohammed re-frained from eating or drinking because of the Ramadan fast. I felt tired and ready to take the train back to Cairo.

"Can we sit somewhere? The sun has zapped my energy," I said, wiping my forehead.

"We will find a place, somewhere outside. We aren't members of the club," he answered. The club was huge and felt luxurious as we walked past the numerous tennis courts and equestrian areas to exit. I was dreaming about being pampered in the club's spa, a complete full body, relaxing massage with pretty, painted, fuchsia toenails. We found a park bench outside. I was hoping that the sightseeing was coming to an end. For some reason, I found it awkward to tell him that it was time for me to head back to Cairo. Part of me wanted to stay longer. I enjoyed his company and liked how the day was unfold-ing. The other side of me dreaded the two-and-half hour train ride back to Cairo.

The Invitation

❝In the middle of every difficulty lies opportunity.❞

– Albert Einstein

It was about four p.m. and the fasting for Ramadan was about to end.

"Mohammed, it is time for me to take the five p.m. train back to Cairo," I said.

"You can't go back so soon," he exclaimed with surprise. "You have to stay for Ramadan dinner. You can't leave Egypt without having a traditional meal. Have you had a traditional meal before?"

My visit to Egypt was in December and Ramadan was in the ninth month of their Islamic lunar calendar. Every day during that month, Muslims spent the daylight hours fasting—forms of spiritual cleansing when Muslims abstained from food, sleep, and sex. Fasting was very important to Muslims because it symbolized loyalty to one's faith.

"No. I want to go back," I replied, even though my mind and heart were battling it out. Deep down, I wanted to meet his family and experience this rich tradition.

"We will have to wait 30 minutes," he told me. "My brother is coming to pick us up. You must stay! I will tell my family you are coming." He pulled out his cell phone.

"I agree to stay, only on the condition that I am on the seven p.m. train back to Cairo," I insisted.

"Great! I have told my aunt and uncle that you are coming for dinner this evening. My parents are away on Hajji to Mecca," he explained.

"Are you sure they are fine with me coming?" I asked. I felt awkward. *Was I to bring a gift? What's their custom?* I wasn't prepared.

"Yes, it is ok," Mohammed smiled. Within 30 minutes, his brother drove up in a beat-up, red-coloured, four-door Toyota. We climbed into the back seat.

"Melanie, this is my brother, Amasis," he said, introducing me.

"Hello, Amasis."

"Hi!" he answered as he snuck a peek from the rear view mirror. He drove at a moderate speed as pop Arabic music blared from the car radio. He looked hip with his dark sunglasses, slimming jeans, and plain gray t-shirt.

We arrived at the home of his relatives, a single-level structure covered in white stucco. It was a quiet and unassuming area like a Canadian middle-income suburb, but I didn't see any of his neighbours around. As I walked through the front door, there was an elderly lady on the couch. Mohammed introduced me in Arabic to his grandma. We smiled at each other and she patted her hand on the seat, gesturing for me to sit beside her. She wore an azure-coloured sebleh, a traditional Egyptian wide, long dress and a headscarf, as pieces of her silvery hair peeked through. She looked like she was in her mid-70s. It was the warmth of her smile that eased my nervousness.

"My grandmother likes your running shoes," Mohammed remarked.

"Shukran," I said with a big smile.

My shoes were streaks of purple with a hint of "glow in the dark" spots. I felt a hodge-podge of mixed emotions: nervous to be in a stranger's home, honoured to be invited, and calm in grandma's presence. In the moments of dead silence, my eyes scanned the mid-sized living room, which also acted as a dining room. The other room I had a glimpse of was the tiny bathroom, with just a small sink and toilet. The simplicity of their home was inviting.

"My aunt and uncle will be here soon," explained Mohammed.

Within minutes they arrived, and he introduced me again. I was surprised to see his uncle dressed in a modern buttoned up shirt and beige trousers, and his aunt wearing a long Egyptian kaftan, called a yelek, over her trousers. Both looked to be in their late 50s. We all smiled at each other, as they spoke very little English. They weren't fazed by my presence, as his aunt quickly disappeared behind a small alcove into what I assumed was the kitchen. She reappeared and disappeared, placing dishes of food on the table. His uncle and brother positioned foldout chairs around the modern dining table. From my observations, the home had tight quarters, but it felt comfy.

Everyone was eager to eat as the fast ended. Mohammed's uncle gestured me to sit at the table.

"We are having grilled rabbit. I hope you like rabbit," he remarked.

"Yes, thanks," I answered, with very slight enthusiasm. The word rabbit conjured an image of *'Thumper'* from the Disney movie *'Bambi.'*

Truthfully, I was afraid to eat meat in Egypt. I couldn't stomach the sight of 'meat' shops located throughout Cairo - tiny wood stalls with raw, bloody meat strewn on old wooden posts, accompanied with buzzing flies in the hot weather. The six of us sat snug around the circular table as we feasted on grilled rabbit, bread, and a vegetable dish. I was pleasantly surprised, the meal was rather tasty. The family spoke in Arabic about the events of the day. Mohammed talked about our visit to the museum, the Corniche along the harbor, and his high school athletic club. Tears welled in my eyes as I reminisced about my family sitting all together enjoying home-cooked dinners. Fortunately, I was so enthralled with the evening that I was not aware of what I was eating.

"My uncle and aunt wanted to know where we met. I told them we just met on the airplane yesterday. They also want to know where else you have visited in Egypt," said Mohammed with a devilish grin.

His aunt attempted to hold back the look of surprise as I saw her raised brows of disapproval.

"I've been to the pyramids, Luxor, Aswan, Abu Simbel, and Sharm el-Sheikh," I said. I acknowledged I had fulfilled my childhood dream of climbing the pyramids.

After dinner, we were served the sweet, flaky pastry called baklava. It was so tasty, my sweet tooth was hankering for seconds, but I held back to be polite. It wasn't long before grandma was the chatty one. Everyone else seemed to be bored. Like a typical Canadian family, they were glued to the television, more interested in hearing the daily news.

However, grandma was fascinated to hear I am Asian, but born in Canada. She could not fathom how Chinese people were living in Canada. She was very curious about snow in my cold country. How would I describe white, fluffy, delicate flakes that fall feather light, but instantly melt in the palm of your hands? I felt a real connection with her, she genuinely wanted to know all about me. She told me stories of her relatives who travelled to China. I realized her family is well-to-do, but still unfamiliar with foreigners.

"It is time to leave for the train station," explained Mohammed. He translated this in Arabic to his grandmother and she nodded in agreement.

I took grandma's soft, wrinkled hands in mine. I looked into her kind eyes, and said, "Shukran, shukran." I felt teary-eyed as she smiled the biggest smile ever.

"Please tell your uncle and aunt I really appreciate their hospitality and thank them for a delicious dinner," I said shaking their hands.

"Mohammed, I truly appreciate you showing me your home town. It is beautiful here. I am happy that you insisted I have Ramadan dinner with your family. I'm glad I got to see another side of Egypt. I want you to know that this has been the best part of my trip. Thank you," I exclaimed.

Truthfully, it was the best part of my trip. I was proud to have the courage to meet Mohammed and I had gained greater confidence.

"I am very happy you liked Alexandria. I am happy you came. Can we keep in touch?" he inquired.

"Yes, we can." We exchanged email addresses. I felt awkward. *Was he going to hug me? Was he going to give me a fond farewell kiss?*

We both continued to wave until I disappeared behind the wall. There was no doubt my day in Alexandria with Mohammed had been a treasured experience.

I felt safe riding in first class with one other male rider. I arrived at Ramses Station at 9:45 p.m., but it felt late. I felt uneasy as I stepped off the train into a poorly lit area. Since I didn't see any taxis around, I dashed back to the Shepheard Hotel.

"Hello, madam. How was your visit to Alexandria?" asked the hotel manager.

"I had a great time. Shukran," I answered.

"Please wait, madam," he said as he disappeared to the back room behind the counter. I gasped. He brought out a big, beautiful floral bouquet mixed with daisies, red roses, and lilies.

"These were delivered today for you, madam," he echoed behind the large bouquet.

For a moment, I thought they were from Mohammed ... my heart skipped a beat. *'Was I developing feelings for this man?'* I thought. The idea quickly evaporated. I opened the note and it read "Happy Birthday, Mel! Love Allan, Alvin, and Andre." I was in tears. They were from not one, but three adoring men – my brothers!

I ordered a bottle of white wine to my room. I sat on the hotel balcony, raising my glass of wine to celebrate my courage to travel solo, as the boats sailed down the Nile. What an amazing, memorable day to celebrate my birthday ... one I would never forget.

Like Jane, the Australian journalist who was never to see her Mumbai prince again, I was never to see Mohammed again – it was, however, a chance encounter that would forever change me. The changes, while imperceptible at first, helped build my confidence and ability to take risks. Moments in time, like these, may not be the big *'fork in the road'*. Rather, they are gentle winds that gently move one towards a new direction ... a better way of being.

Take risks when you travel, just make sure they are calculated risks.

www.gutsyladytravel.com/www.gutsyladytravel.ca

Chapter Four

Gutsy Mom

"The more a daughter knows the details of her mother's life –
without flinching or whining – the stronger the daughter."

– Anita Diamant, "The Red Tent"

My mother is an anomaly. She is tiny, but tough. A survivor ... literally.

Mui was born in China about 1930. I say "about" because we're not really sure just how old she is.

My mother came from the time when the horrors of the Japanese invasion of China played out in all of its brutality, in 1937.

During the Japanese invasion, they quickly captured all key Chinese ports and industrial centres, including cities such as the Chinese capital Nanking and Shanghai; CCP and KMT forces continued resisting. In a horrifying conflict, both sides used "scorched earth" tactics. Massacres and atrocities were common. The most infamous came after the fall of Nanking in December 1937 when Japanese troops slaughtered an estimated 300,000 civilians and raped 80,000 women, which was utterly sickening. The rape of Nanking (as it came to be known) was one of the most terrible atrocities of World War II. Thousands of

Chinese were killed in the indiscriminate bombing of cities and villages by the Jap-anese air force. There were also savage reprisals carried out against Chinese peasants in retaliation for attacks by partisans who waged a guerrilla war against the invader, ambushing supply columns and attacking isolated units. Warfare of this nature led, by the war's end, to an estimated 10 to 20 million Chinese civilian deaths. Prisoners who were not raped or tortured, were often used for bayonet practice by the Japanese.

My grandparents and aunt were among those who were killed.

This was the China in which my mother was born. Her family were poor peasants, farmers who had very little education, and probably no political affiliations as yet, while their government was busy playing their cat and mouse games. The poor were the ones who suffered in their war-torn country.

When my mother was about nine, the Japanese invaded their peaceful village, targeting their bombing on the huts and buildings so they could inflict as much death and damage as possible. As the bombs were dropped, her home was hit and she watched in horror as her mother, father, and older sister were incinerated. Fortunately, my mother's older brother grabbed her by the hand and dragged her to safety. Life had been difficult prior to the death of her parents, and after they were killed, each day was a struggle to survive. Starvation wasn't the only problem. The lack of employment opportunities, disease, and illnesses made life in China a brutal existence.

After my grandparents were killed, my mother was taken care of by her older brothers. Although they did their best, the lack of money and the strain of caring for a little girl was simply too much for them. Unfortunately, the journey from the rural village to Hong Kong, although not expensive, was too pricey to spend money sending my mother, so they came up with a plan. They decided that the best place with the most opportunities for my mother was living with distant relatives in Hong Kong. My mother would be taken to Hong

Kong on a small sampan (fishing boat) and, in exchange for the several week journey, she would cook for the lone owner of the boat.

"NO, NO, NO! I am not going! I want to stay here with you! I don't care if I have nothing to eat," my mother yelled as tears streamed down her face. She was begging and pleading with her oldest brother to let her stay. She was still grieving and devastated from the loss of her parents and the truth was, death due to starvation was lurking throughout the village. The reality of it was that she witnessed many deaths from starvation. When we were young, this was her way to get my brothers and me to eat all of our food: "You know, if you lived in China, there's nothing to eat and you are so hungry, you would be eating bird poop." We thought it was hysterically funny and resisted even more. It was fact.

Now as a wiser, mature woman, I understand what people do for survival. I am more respectful of locals in other countries. I was humbled when I heard my excited Indian server in Coimbatore tell me he had surpassed his first year out of his five-year work probation, and when I saw a family of four living on just a piece of plank supported by stilts behind the Hilton Hotel in Lombok, Indonesia.

Upon arriving in Hong Kong, my mother stayed with her so called 'godparents' and three young children. She was a temporary nanny until she was old enough to look for a job. Shortly after, she was able to find employment in a factory, where, despite the low wages and long working hours, she enjoyed her job. There were other girls her age and status and, probably for the first time in her life, she was able to have a sense of freedom and fun.

After several years working in the Hong Kong factory sewing, my mother decided it was time to move on and so she applied (and was hired) as a servant for a general physician and his wife, a headmaster of an English-speaking school. This was one of her first experiences with a Caucasian. Although she was still very young and inexperienced, my mom, once again, showed initiative and excelled in her job. Since labour was so cheap in Hong Kong, the headmaster had one servant per task and my mom's only task was to shop for the day's meals. Each day, she'd step into the chauffeur-driven car and would be driven to the food markets. Since there was limited refrigeration and the household (including the servants) was large, she became very adept at not only identifying and choosing the freshest fruits, vegetables, and other staples, but also at bargaining and purchasing at the best prices possible.

Once again, my mother had found a position where she was very happy and found the work satisfying. The headmaster was very kind and became a sort of mother figure to her. The husband was kind and caring.

In the fall of 1959, my mother's godmother approached her with an interesting proposition.

"Would you be interested in being married? I have a good friend in Victoria, BC, Canada, who is a sort of matchmaker. Her husband is close friends with a very successful farmer who is in need of a wife," asked her godmother.

"I don't know. What information do you have about this man?" questioned my mother, with uncertainty.

"I am not quite sure. I will write to Mrs. Leong and ask," answered her godmother. She wasn't completely enthusiastic either because it meant losing her free babysitter.

In a matter of weeks, snail mail arrived with a photo of a man sitting on a beach blanket in his swim trunks, posing like Arnold Schwarzenegger with flexed arms. *'Wow! What a muscular body,'* she thought. She now became rather delighted.

This was her chance, my mother thought. After all, she was 22-years-old and in Hong Kong her prospects were limited. Did she want to be a servant all her life, never to move up in the world? No. She knew this was an opportunity of a lifetime – a chance for a better, more enriched life.

Canada, like the United States, was the pinnacle of success in the minds of poor servants like my mother. It was known as "The Gold Mountain"

(Gum Shan) because many Chinese who immigrated to British Columbia became rich from the gold that was mined. The fact was, his grandfather had become wealthy from mining the gold in the rivers of British Columbia. In order to be rich, all they had to do was pan for gold and nuggets would appear as the water washed away the sand. It was truly a dream come true for a poor girl with few prospects in Hong Kong.

But when she mentioned the opportunity to the head master, she was not as enthusiastic as my mother had hoped.

"Do you understand that it's very different in Canada than here in Hong Kong?" she asked. "In Canada it is cold ... very cold. The living conditions are too harsh. The people aren't like here in Hong Kong – even the Chinese. You're probably not going to like it there. For heaven's sake ... the people wear shoes. Even farmers wear shoes," she exclaimed in a worrisome tone. 'Even farmers wear shoes' was about the biggest slam that someone could say in Hong Kong.

So what did my mother do? She did what any self-respecting young Chinese woman living in Hong Kong in the 1950s would do: She went to a temple to consult a fortune teller.

Kau Cim, or Chinese fortune telling, is an ancient practice in China, and especially in Hong Kong. It can be traced back to the Jin Dynasty in the third century. Many of the fortune tellers used Kau Cim sticks made of bamboo to predict the future. My mother consulted an elderly fortune teller who, although he was blind, foresaw my mother's future. He used the powerful sticks to make his predictions.

"Ahhh!" said the old man with a big, long sigh. His head nodded up and down.

My mother instantly knew it wasn't going to be a good reading. Unfortunately for my mother, the white-bearded fortune teller echoed the sentiments of the head master.   He predicted that she would be unhappy and if she ventured to Canada, she'd hate living there facing much hardship. Clearly a master of his work, he told her the number of children (at least three and maybe four maximum), their birth order (a daughter and two or three younger sons), and their personalities – and his predictions turned out to be crystal clear with precise accuracy. He knew that my mother would ignore his advice as well as her employer's, and she would make the trip to Canada to meet and marry the man who was destined to be my father. And that's exactly what she did.

My mom flew into Victoria, BC, arriving on New Year's Eve, 1959. She rang in the next year in a promising country with a brand new life – one vastly different from the last two decades in China.

When my mother arrived, she was met by Mrs. Leong, the local match-maker, and her husband. Mrs. Leong was the 1950s larger-than-life version of match.com. She was proud of her perfect record – four love matches made in heaven. Already things were off to a wobbly start. My mother was disappointed and upset that her husband-to-be wasn't at the airport welcoming her with loving arms. According to my mother, Mrs. Leong made up some lame excuse why my father didn't show up.

She met my father, grandmother, and the rest of the family a couple of days later at his home. When she met my father, she was disenchanted. Was the photo altered? This man was 19 years older and shy. He was also crippled, walking with a bad limp in both legs. Almost as bad was the fact that, although it was my father's house, she learned that she would have to live with his mother and his single sister. Often she cried tears of sorrow and sadness, regretting that she didn't listen to her headmaster and fortune teller. She would be starting her new married life living in a house with two other women who were vastly different in upbringing, culture, and beliefs than she was.

This was not the fairytale she had hoped for, and it certainly wasn't how she dreamt her new life would be. But she had no choice – she had to stay because she didn't have the money to return to Hong Kong, and not knowing the language, would be unable to find employment. She was stuck … forever.

My mother decided to make the best of the situation and follow through with the arranged marriage. Wearing a borrowed Western-style wedding dress, my parents were married in the middle of January 1960. My mom, dad, and two other women all lived in the two-bedroom bungalow that my father had purchased. The two worlds clashed despite their similar cultural background.

Although all were Chinese, culturally, they were extremely different. The Chinese from the old country are so much more traditional and hang onto their old beliefs and customs. Chinese Canadians, on the other hand, are more Westernized and easygoing. During the 1960s, many Chinese immigrants living in Canada didn't assimilate into the Western culture. In fact, if they entered into a Caucasian marriage, they could be ostracized and even disinherited by their own families. However, the 'Eng' family went against the grain. The puny Asian community of Victoria shunned our family for having 'coloured' (Caucasian) relatives.

Thus began my mother's new life in Canada: The 'Golden Mountain', a land and country that my mother never called home. So intensely did my mother feel the alienation from her new family that she never even tried to fit into the Westernized culture of Canada – to the extent that she never learned to speak English. Thus, when I was born in 1960, I too never learned English until I started school, skipping kindergarten and starting in first grade.

Freedom to choose what you do, where you travel, and how you live should never be taken for granted. If you don't take advantage of those freedoms, circumstances, and opportunities, even if it is not an arranged marriage, this will dictate your direction in life.

Be bold. Be willing to take gutsy risks.

Chapter Five

Tractor Dad

❝It is easier for a father to have children than for children to have a real father. ❞

– Pope John XXIII

My dad, a second generation Chinese-Canadian farmer, always seemed to be an intensely quiet man. He was born in Victoria, BC, like his mother. However, his dad and his uncle came by ship from China to Victoria in their early teens. No doubt, my dad preferred to be gone from our house since he was torn between his new Chinese wife, his mother, and sister. It wasn't a very happy home life for him. From my early childhood, he wasn't around much, seeming to prefer to be at work or to spend his free time gambling in Fan Tan Alley (Victoria's Chinatown).

He also, as I mentioned, was crippled. Years earlier, he'd been ploughing in the field and somehow the tractor turned over on the embankment, pinning him beneath it. When he was finally rescued, my father spent eight months in the hospital recovering from his injuries, although he would be forever crippled, walking with a bad limp for the rest of his life.

It was my grandparents' belief that no woman would ever want to marry a crippled man, especially a farmer with a menial job.

My dad never talked about what happened that tragic day. I was ashamed to admit to my classmates that my father was crippled and that he was a farmer. I wanted so badly to fit in at school and to be accepted. I felt like a freak being the only Asian kid in the entire school living on a hillbilly farm.

Unfortunately, any happiness that my parents might have experienced was probably doomed from the start. My mother was dissatisfied with my father and she showed it daily. My father wasn't the smart, successful farmer that she'd dreamed about. He was 19 years her senior, crippled, with a farm that barely made a living. We were, in fact, living at poverty level in a tiny two-bedroom house, with women my mom loathed. Despite my father owning the house, my grandmother ruled it with an iron fist and frequently turned on my mother.

Finally, when I was about five, my father built a new house on the farm. My mom broke free from the bondage of the in-law. My father wasn't the wanderlust like me. The furthest place he travelled was Vancouver, BC, but, there was a private, adventurous side to him. I was told that in his youth, he was 'Speed Racer', with a passion to drive stock cars.

He was definitely a homebody, content in nature while riding his red tractor. He and I were both shy introverts, but polar opposites when travelling the world. Beneath my shyness, I had a wild and adventurous spirit from playing on the farm. I remembered the sweet and fond childhood memories as I felt the cool and soft earthy mud squish between my bare toes in the lettuce patch, and the fun of mastering our own 'Evel Knieval' (a 70s American daredevil) stuntman bike jumps only to land on the cushy earth. Oh! And the glorious freedom to wander into late evenings.

I felt I never really knew who my father was. There were no warm hugs or heartfelt words of 'I love you'. My father was eventually completely wheelchair bound and was then placed in a convalescent home. He was content to read my captivating worldly postcards plastered with colourful foreign stamps.

Regardless if your parents are alive, passed, or you don't have a relationship, they did their best as they knew how. Honoring them will always give you peace.

www.gutsyladytravel.com/www.gutsyladytravel.ca

Chapter Six

A Requited Love

" What we all want in life, to travel, fall in love and be happy. "

– Anonymous

When you're single, the chances are you will meet someone along the way during your travels. Meeting people from foreign lands always carries with it a sliver of mystery and, for the most part, sexy accents.

While there are plenty of examples of meeting the love of your life abroad, there are equal (or greater) examples of relationships that are born, blossom, and die in short order.

Love doesn't always have the fairytale ending.

This is something my friend Sophie had to learn the hard way.

Sophie was at a music concert in Frankfurt, Germany years ago. She was not a conservative gal, but not one of those totally free spirits either. Her background in international marketing gave her a global perspective, but her proper British upbringing, being conservative, also kept her a bit innocent.

She loved music and had been to many concerts in her lifetime. Seeing one of her favorite bands while on assignment in Germany was a dream come true. That dream, as it turns out, was about to ramp up tenfold.

During the final set, she was dancing easily to the music when her heart suddenly dropped upon seeing a blond-haired guy who was gently smiling and staring directly at her. This guy, who wasn't her usual type, was about six feet tall with a lean build and blazing blue eyes. She tried to dismiss his attentions, but couldn't shake them off right away.

As quickly as the concert started, it also ended. She turned one last time to see those steely-blue eyes and he was gone …

She shrugged it off and decided to go to an after-party at a club about six blocks away, with her friend Bianca.

The after-party, which was held at a famed rock 'n' roll hotel, was littered with handsome guys and drinks galore. In your mid 20s and 30s this type of atmosphere was sexually energized and, to Sophie, it was no different than a designer shoe store.

About an hour into the festivities, one of these Jimmy Choos tapped Sophie's shoulder and said that his friend wanted to meet her. Now, when one guy asks on behalf of another, a red flag usually goes up. *'Why can't he say hello himself?'* she wondered.

Inquisitive, she followed the guy across the club to see what was in store. The hair looked vaguely familiar, but he was not facing her when she approached. This guy's buddy touched him on the shoulder and he turned around.

It was smouldering blue eyes!

Now, from a concert with 3,000 people and with dozens of after parties, the odds of seeing the same guy twice is pretty uncommon. Even rarer was seeing the same person with whom there was an initial interest.

"My name is Roger," he said in an American accent as he got up and gestured to Sophie to sit down.

She sat, transfixed, and the two started talking – and talking. In fact, the bar was closing, and they took a stroll along a quiet boulevard and continued talking until the glow of the morning sun began to peek over the horizon.

Their connection felt like they had already met in a previous lifetime.

American Roger, however, had to fly back to New York later that day, so they grabbed his stuff and headed for a coffee until he was due to be picked up.

It seemed they could just talk about anything and everything at a deeper level.

They exchanged emails and phone numbers and promised to keep in contact.

For some reason, unbeknownst to her, Sophie never heard from Roger again.

When travelling, sometimes chance encounters and fleeting moments anchor into something that grows. Other times, like two ships that pass in the night, a relationship may be snuffed out instantly. A year passed. Sophie was offered a job in New York and decided to take it – she was, after all, single and ready for a new adventure. She had just about forgotten about American Roger.

Upon landing at JFK, she was reunited with Bianca, who had moved to New York a mere three months earlier. She suggested they go for brunch at a cool West Village spot. Hungry and tired, Sophie agreed.

The spot was quaint, with a French vibe and equally small portions of French food. They ordered, sat, and caught up about their recent adventures. It felt good for the pair to be reunited.

Then Bianca's face dropped.

"What's up?" Sophie said.

"I think you should turn around and see who just walked in the door," she told Sophie.

Sophie turned, her eyes caught Roger's, and her heart dropped again.

There are over eight million people in New York City. With a metro area the size of a small country, what were the odds that she'd see blazing blue-eyed Roger?

Bianca asked if Sophie was ok as she was visibly shaking. Sophie saw it as a sign.

Was it fate? What powers in the universe could possibly take these two people and thrust them together not once, but three times? Sophie turned back to Bianca, wearing the expression of a mannequin.

"Are you ok? You look like you saw a ghost." Bianca asked.

Sophie could not move, speak, or react. She saw that Roger was with a longhaired brunette, but that didn't stop him from constantly looking over at Sophie every chance he got.

For 30 uncomfortable minutes, the two stole glances every few moments … not knowing if they should get up and say hello, or look down at their petite French meals. After an equally awkward period of time, just like at the concert, Sophie looked up … and he was gone.

"That's it," Sophie said to Bianca. "I can't see this dude again. It is simply too freaky. I mean, in Germany, I was whisked away into the fastest romance of my life … seeing him here again, pulled those almost forgotten feelings straight to my heart. What's wrong with me?" she asked.

"Sophie," Bianca said, "I can't explain it, but if you ever see him again, do something."

"No worries. New York is way too big for that."

What we say to ourselves isn't always what we believe. In Sophie's heart, she longed for a chance to talk with Roger … to see if the girl he was with was a serious thing. Heck, maybe it was his sister!

She chuckled to herself and thought, "Get a grip, girl."

A week later, Sophie's friend Simon, from the London office, was in town. Eager to go out, she offered to give him an English girl's tour of New York City. After the tour, they'd explore New York's nightlife.

After visiting the Statue of Liberty and a museum, they went back to the New York office and checked up on the tasks they avoided during the day. One of the benefits of working internationally is, your boss is rarely nearby to check in on you.

That night, the two headed to a Lower East Village bar with a definitive rock 'n' roll vibe. They ordered drinks, sat, and took in the scenery and the array of hipsters flooding through the doors. The local band was good, the place wasn't overly crowded, and that would prove to be fortuitous on this night ….

There he was – again!

'Not again!' she screamed at herself in her head. How on earth can this be happening? For a moment, Sophie pondered if this guy was stalking her or if he had a twin brother. He didn't see her straight away and she decided to move slightly out of his field of vision to collect her thoughts.

Simon noticed her change and asked, "Everything ok, love?"

"Um … yeah … there is someone here, I uh …."

"No worries. Old boyfriend?" he correctly surmised.

Sophie lowered her head and shrugged her shoulders.

"Listen, I'll watch our drinks. Why don't you go say hello? I've got your back."

Sophie's mind was spinning and she decided to call Bianca for some advice.

As she walked outside to call Bianca, she rounded the corner outside the door; it would be quieter there. She took a deep breath, pulled out her phone, and began to dial. After she finished dialing the number she looked up, and Roger was standing there ... smiling softly at her.

"It's good to see you," he said. "How long have you and your boyfriend been together?" he asked.

"We're not together – we are just friends," Sophie said, but before she could go into further details or delve into the conversation any further, Simon came out and announced that he wanted to leave. (It turned out Simon had a secret crush on Sophie and was hoping to halt any conversation between her and Roger.)

Sophie felt like raising her hands in the air as a sign of defeat, but nodded at Simon and said, "Ok."

Not being her normally calm and cool self, Sophie was at a loss for words and didn't even realize her call had connected with Bianca. "I will see you around," she told Roger.

Simon carefully took her by the arm and escorted her to a cab. They got in and headed back to Manhattan.

And see him around she did – for two years these chance meetings with Roger continued to happen.

On one occasion, her work threw a Christmas party lunch at a bar in Soho (an artists' neighborhood in Lower Manhattan, New York City), and who happened to walk in at two p.m. with a friend?

Old blue eyes.

The way they looked at each other never changed, but it seemed their timing was always off and they could never rekindle those magical, precious moments when they first met in Germany.

The one thing Sophie thought about countlessly, and craved the most, was to get lost in endless hours of conversation with him again. To be in his arms again ... to feel time stand still as they laughed effortlessly, loved openly, and relished the timeless nuances of being together.

Was he her soulmate? Did she even believe in such things? Sophie, like many of us, craved the connection, the chemistry, and the selfless love of being with someone who is more than special .... Yes, she actually did believe in soulmates.

Roger may have been it.

But she would never know the truth. She would never discover if he was "Mr. Right" or "Mr. Right Now".

She would never see him again.

Of all the mysteries of travel and developing courage, none compare to love. It can't be bought, traded, or bargained with. It just happens.

If there is a chance for love, take the risk.

www.gutsyladytravel.com/www.gutsyladytravel.ca

Chapter Seven

New Plateaus, Higher Elevations

*"A traveller am I, and a navigator, and every day
I discover a new region within my soul."*

– Kahlil Gibran

For some, travelling brings love. For others, it gives them an entirely different perspective on the world.

For me, personally, travelling really helped build my confidence, which I relayed into my day-to-day life after I returned to San Francisco from Egypt. It was like my self-esteem was ignited within.

When I overcame my fear of dining solo, I felt triumphant. I was on top of the world. I believed I could do anything and everything. I wouldn't have experienced this if I was on a group tour or if I had told family and friends that I was travelling solo. I was saved from the "peer pressure" or "comments from the peanut gallery". I don't deny I was terrified, but this trip allowed me to reflect on who I was and who I wanted to be. I wanted to be more confident.

When I returned to work, I was dreading the "*same old, same old*" of work. I was the "*yes*" person, who didn't talk back or voice my opinions; too afraid to speak out and speak up. I worked for the telephony company for over a year and found out that the last executive assistant hired made more money than I, even though she was less skilled and had fewer years under her belt. Then there was the Executive Assistant to the President, who earned more in salary, but was barely knowledgeable in her skills, often relying on others such as myself. I wasn't happy and felt the whole situation was unfair, but I couldn't quit as I was a Canadian on a U.S. working visa.

However, I returned from Egypt a changed woman. I felt more confident. I chose to voice my dissatisfaction with my CFO boss. I found a quiet time to talk to him when he was in a good mood. I took a deep breath, gathered my newly found confidence, and jumped in.

"Don, I have worked at this company for just over a year now. I feel I have more skills than most of the executive assistants here. I have worked as an executive assistant in various positions for over 20 years, which is more than any of them. I assisted the president with his travel issues when his assistant didn't know how. I found over $1,000 in unauthorized expenses from one of the salesmen, and recently handled disgruntled shareholders' calls for the public relations department. I feel I deserve a raise."

I said it all with conviction, even though I felt my face turning red and was sweating underneath. I could tell he was surprised, but he knew what I presented was true.

"Let me think about it. I will let you know in a couple of days."

"Good. Thanks." I walked out confidently. I knew he had to go to bat for me and talk to his boss. A couple of days passed and Don called me.

"Melanie, can you please come in when you're finished with what you are doing?"

"Sure." I instantly knew what it was about. I knocked on his door and walked in, closing the door behind me.

"Have a seat," he directed me to the leather chair across from his desk. I was nervous and the moment of truth was about to be revealed.

"I have spoken with Rich about your raise. I agree with what you said and believe you deserve a raise. As of June, you will get a raise of …. In addition, we are willing to support you in getting your green card." I was elated and was doing the happy dance inside. Even with my newfound confidence, I was shocked that I got what I deserved.

"Thank you, Don." I was beaming inside and out. I finally mustered the courage to ask for what I wanted. I was victorious. I was extremely proud of my accomplishment. I did it, and I felt my inner strength rising to greater heights.

The Turquoise Blue Water

" It's better to look back on life and say: "I can't believe I did that," than to look back and say: "I wish I did that. "

– Unknown

At a later date, I was showing my Egypt photos to friends at work.

"OMG!!! I can't believe you travelled there on your own! Do you remember me telling you that Egypt isn't safe for women just before you left? Weren't you scared?" Sharon, my co-worker, shook her head in disbelief.

"Yes, I was scared at the beginning, but all these wonderful self-discoveries revealed themselves along the way. Can you believe my biggest challenge was dining alone? Remember, we talked about this before I left. But once I overcame that fear, I felt I could conquer anything."

"That's amazing! You're brave. I don't know what I would have done if I had to do it alone." We turned to another picture.

"Oh, my God! Where is this beautiful place? It's stunning," she said, pointing to the brilliant blue water.

"That is Sharm el-Sheikh, the beach resort town that's an hour plane ride from Cairo."

"Did you go swimming?"

I instantly cringed.

"No," I replied, sheepishly.

Sharon asked, "Why not?"

"I don't know how to swim. Actually, I had a near drowning experience as a kid at the local lake."

"I'm surprised. I can't believe you can't swim."

That evening, I reminisced about the little, turquoise fish I saw at Sharm el-Shiekh. Of all the beautiful waters I've visited in the world, from Bali to the Caribbean, Sharm el-Shiekh takes the prize. Every single time I left those places, my heart ached with melancholy. It was another agonizing moment where I thought – I could have learned to swim, I should have learned to swim. I was saddened that my deep desire to have fun in the water was hindered by my fear of it. Now, I return stronger and with greater confidence. I envision higher hopes about myself. I wonder whether I have it in me to make a fifth attempt at swimming lessons. The truth is, each time at swimming lessons, I slowly improved. I could float on my front and I felt comfortable being in waist deep water. I began seeing the positives of it all.

Within a month, I had decided to take swimming lessons again … at the ripe age of 40. I concluded that my chances would be greater if I took private swimming lessons. I phoned various swim clubs and organizations. I felt it was important to have a coach I could connect with, who really would understand what I went through. I interviewed two women and one man. They were all in their 20s except for Cathy. I met them all personally to see if they were the right fit for me. I also wanted a senior instructor. The instructor I chose needed the qualifications, the extensive training and testing, to be a senior instructor. Also, I wanted someone who would not only empower me, but also encourage and inspire me at the same time. Cathy was the perfect instructor with over 10 years as a senior mentor. She was in her late 30s, a heavy-set gal, but muscular. I signed up and our agreement was for two classes per week until I learned to swim. Living in sunny California meant swim lessons were outside.

I was feeling excited and confident. The weekend before my first lesson, I purchased some swim goggles and a new swimsuit. I was so excited to start that I showed up 15 minutes early for my initial session! I was taken aback when I saw Cathy dressed in a white sleeveless T-shirt with red shorts and flip-flops. I thought, *"She will probably change shortly, since I'm early."*

"Hi, Melanie! Let's start by getting in the pool," she said.

I hopped in. She wasn't getting in and I was puzzled.

"Aren't you getting in?" I asked.

"Nope! That's not how I teach. I can see you much better from here," she said confidently.

I wondered how she could teach when she wasn't even in the pool. In my opinion, she should have been in the water next to me. This new concept was foreign to me. My level of confidence deflated. Before I could ask another question, Cathy said, "I want you to show me some basic strokes. Can you float?"

"Just a bit," I answered, timidly.

"Show me," she said in a loud voice.

I attempted it and ended up floundering as I splashed and thrashed.

"Try it again. I need you to relax first," she said louder.

"I find it difficult to relax," I answered.

"Ok. Then do your best." It wasn't long before class ended. I was relieved.

"You did well today. I will see you on Thursday," she stated, with some disappointment.

"Yeah, see you then," I replied with my head held low. I doubted whether I would return. How can she teach me when she's standing way up there, five feet above me? The next five to six classes were the same with little progress. I felt deflated, frustrated, ready to quit for the fifth time! Meanwhile, two lanes over, a lean and athletic teenager was instructing eight-year-olds.

"Show me airplane. Good! Now show me soldier," he told the kids. I was embarrassed that they were learning faster than I was.

At my eighth class, Cathy said, "You almost have it. Just move your right arm a little further back as you slightly tilt your body to the left. Then bring your right arm up and over."

I made several attempts, each attempt ending in frustration. I felt like a total failure, just like the other four previous shots. I felt frustration; I just could not get it. I was ready to give up again, but chose to continue on as I reminisced about the turquoise blue fish in Egypt. That was exactly what I needed! Sometimes we need to be reminded why we want to do something. Finally, I had my "aha" moment – I did it!

"Great, Melanie! Yes, you've done it!!!" Cathy shouted with her arms held high.

I was jumping up and down in triumph.

It made me think of the cheerleaders in our lives, encouraging us even when we are ready to throw in the towel. I am grateful that Cathy was my cheerleader and wasn't going to give up on me.

In the 2000 Olympics, Eric Moussambani of Equatorial Guinea swam in a 50 metre (160 foot) long Olympic-size pool. He wasn't there to set an Olympic record. He was from a developing country and never received all the bells and whistles of sponsorship or technical coaching. He taught himself how to swim in a lake only eight months before the Olympics. He had never seen an Olympic-size swimming pool, let alone dipped his toes into one. Before a crowd of 17,000, and 30 metres from the finish, they roared for this courageous underdog. In 2012, he was appointed coach of the national swimming squad of Equatorial Guinea, empowering others.[1]

The important lesson for me was, most of us have cheerleaders in our lives who will not give up on us. Often, it is our limiting beliefs that we can't do this or can't do that hold us back. We tend to give up too soon and too fast. I was ready to wave the white flag in defeat. I was too embarrassed and ashamed to tell others that I was taking swimming lessons for the fifth time. When we choose to change our perspective (like Eric and myself), that empowers us and in turn, we become a cheerleader for others.

Three years later, I fulfilled my dream of snorkeling amongst the array of fishes at the Great Barrier Reef in Australia.

I had come a long way.

All travel contains more uncertainty than certainty.
Combining persistence with flexibility is the key to success.

www.gutsyladytravel.com/www.gutsyladytravel.ca

Chapter Eight

Courageous Lioness

"Do not follow where the path may lead. Go instead where there is no path and leave a trail."

– Ralph Waldo Emerson

C ourage can mean so many things to so many different people. Often, in fact, we don't even realize that it takes courage to improve our life. We just see a goal, a want, a need, and then figure out a way to get it. As a young kid, my goal was sweets.

There was a closet sized grocery store near our house that was owned by a jolly, silvery white-haired widow, Mrs. Palmer. Although I was shy, she never seemed to just look through or ignore me, as did many of the other adults. The vast majority of her customers were school children. Her store was heavenly with 95% stocked with Cracker Jacks popcorn, gigantic gumballs, pixie sticks, sour berries, Sweet Tarts, and potato chips. Her store was sandwiched between our elementary school and the ball park. Business was good. I was one of her best customers. Oh, yes! The very first time I tasted candy, I became enthralled with it. It was such a change over our daily meals of plain rice and boring vegetables. A sweet change, indeed.

Living on a farm, we had plenty of vegetables, but they tasted bland. Candy became my love of choice, so to sweeten my addiction I needed money to buy candy. Across the street from the farm was a baseball field where, during the spring and summer, Little League games were played several times a week. I needed cash to support my addiction. Maybe the people sitting in the stands would be interested in buying fresh bunches of carrots that my father's farm grew. So my brothers and I grabbed several bunches of carrots, carefully washed them off, and ran across the street to offer them to people.

"Would you like to buy a bunch of carrots from my father's farm?" I asked, shyly.

"Nope," the woman waved me off.

"Would you like to buy some carrots?" I asked the man two seats away.

"What?" his eyes steadily focused on his son holding the bat.

"Would you like to buy ...?" I raised my voice slightly.

"No, thanks! Come on, Johnny!" he clapped his hands as he cheered his son on.

It was a tough sell. The hardest part was gathering the courage to ask, but I desperately wanted candy.

To my surprise, several people DID want garden fresh carrots, and bought them all. And so the cash began to flow. Enough to satisfy our craving temporarily, and if it was a good day, enough for a root beer soda. We were elated.

But running back and forth was not efficient. So I dragged my little, plastic table out to the edge of the yard and set up a carrot stand with a little handmade sign: CARROTS FOR SALE. Once again, people bought the carrots and we sold out. This was the beginning of my little vegetable stand enterprise. The whole family got into the business. My mom picked the vegetables and we added more and more varieties to the stand. The tiny, plastic kid's table could no longer support the wide variety of vegetables, so my father built a larger table, and eventually, a stand with a roof on it.

And so that was how our vegetable stand grew. Each summer we'd have more vegetables – even reselling pumpkins from the neighbours down the road – and we'd make more and more money. Within a couple of years, we went from poverty level to making over four figures a day with our little vegetable stand. By this time, I was able to buy as much candy as I could eat.

But the vegetable stand wasn't the only entrepreneurial way that I made money to buy my passion. I also discovered a girl in school who loved candy as much as I did and, unfortunately, she wasn't allowed to have it. She did, however, have lunch money. Lunch money was the same as gold in our world, so I made a deal with her. I'd buy her candy at the store and bring it to school, and she'd pay me from her lunch money. This worked well for both of us. I'd charge a premium and was able to buy my own candy from her lunch money. Enterprising at its finest!

Thinking of entrepreneurial business ventures is easy.
Developing the persistence and patience to pull them off is what separates
failure from success.

www.gutsyladytravel.com/www.gutsyladytravel.ca

Chapter Nine

Beyond Courage

**" You were born with wings, why *prefer to* crawl
through life? "**

– Rumi

It requires practice to become courageous. When we repeat it often enough, it becomes second nature to us. It requires courage to acknowledge the fears, whether it is black, creepy spiders, or giving voice to how we truly feel. What is fearful to one person, comes naturally to another. We have fears about what others think. It is the dreaded ego mind of "what will they think" that holds us back from living the life we truly want. More often than not, we become good at beating up on ourselves. We have constantly compared ourselves to others for so many years that we have forgotten to celebrate our own accomplishments over time. We need to be kind and compassionate to ourselves.

Our willingness to talk about our fears requires being open and vulnerable. Some of us grew up in families where we were not to talk about our family problems and, God forbid, the family "secrets". These issues keep us stuck, a prisoner of our minds in mental solitary confinement. Often, social conditioning teaches us to be dependent rather than independent.

Once we step into being courageous, we see ourselves in a different light. We possess a greater inner strength that we have never experienced before. We feel better about ourselves and possess greater confidence. There is new freedom and an ignited passion.

A few years after my Egypt trip, I felt even more *stuck* in my career. I felt at a loss about my career path, hopping from job to job, spending no more than two years at the same position. I couldn't quite pin it down. I wasn't happy and didn't know what my life purpose was. Yeah, the high paying jobs paid the bills and allowed me to travel, but I wasn't passionate about what I did. I had an abundance of excuses ranging from placing blame on my demanding 'boss,' to the workload was too 'much' even though I didn't even have to work overtime. I was dissatisfied and miserable. I was good at pointing fingers at others, but never at me.

At my last job as an executive assistant, I recall the day I had a job review after being employed for one year. My employer was happy and proud of my accomplishment in learning a job within a few months in spite of there being no one to train me. A raise and praise for a job well done left me feeling dissatisfied. When I asked for more money than was offered, they said no.

I was complaining about this on the phone to Allan, my younger brother. "I just got a good job review, but I'm not happy," I said.

"That's great they gave you a good review, considering how the economy is right now," he replied.

"Yeah, but I wanted more money. They wouldn't give me a higher raise. I'm pissed. I hate my job," I remarked.

"You have always said that about all your jobs," he told me.

"I know." I acknowledged I was good at fault-finding with others.

"Well, I have something to ask you. I have been meaning to ask you this for a while now. Would you be willing to buy our stores (retail stores)?" he questioned.

"What do you mean?" I asked.

"Andre and I don't want to be in the kitchen retail business anymore," he explained.

"Five stores! I don't know if I can manage one on my own, let alone five! Why do you want to ask me? I don't know a thing about retail business," I said.

"You are always griping about your jobs and how you hate them. You need a change. We will help you," he said. The truth stings. He was right. I was complaining a lot.

"Let me think about it," I mumbled.

"Fine, let me know soon as I will be putting the businesses up for sale with a realtor," he said.

I sat there in disbelief. I had a tidal wave of emotions – running high with excitement, and dropping deep into fear. My brother gave me only a month to decide, but I wanted several months because this was a life-changer. I wanted to ensure that I was going to make the right decision. In hindsight, it was good that I was given a short period of time, otherwise I would be waiting forever to decide about the 'what ifs'. It was similar to my Egypt trip where I had to decide quickly if I was going to meet Mohammed in Alexandria. We know that highly successful business people take risks and make decisions quickly. They don't wait for the right time ... there's never a right time. Acting boldly develops your 'courageous muscles' better than overthinking.

The weeks that followed were filled with much doubt and uncertainty; I was at a crossroads. I was stressed having to keep it a secret until I made a decision, and I feared the backlash and the onslaught of negativity from family and friends. I wasn't able to eat and sleep as a result of this stress.

This was a 'no brainer', the scale of cons far outweighed the pros, hands down. I would be trapped in 12 - 14 hour days with no time for vacation. I would be a "Jackie of all trades" as president, HR, accountant, and janitor, plus I needed to fork over my life savings to invest in the business. Plagued with thousands of negative and positive thoughts, my mind was in a state of San Francisco fog: '*I am not good enough to be a business owner; I am not smart enough to run the financial aspects of the business; I am too shy to talk to customers; I don't know anything about Human Resources, etc.*' I was good at beating up on myself: 'I'm too this, I'm too that, I'm not good at ....'

It sounded all too depressing, but buried deep down, my heart craved something new and different. Too many decades of the same old boring job as an executive assistant left me uninspired and unfulfilled. I wasn't happy, whether working for six week vacations or working for large corporations listed on NASDAQ. I was tired of pretending that life was rosy. My passion for life desperately needed to be reignited within. However, simultaneously, I feared failure.

I received endless negative remarks ranging from, 'Are you crazy, you know nothing about owning a retail store?' to 'It's challenging for a single woman to run a business.' The doom and gloom comments came too late for me to change my mind. In fact, I felt depressed and angry as I received little emotional support other than from my brothers. There is also that infamous glass ceiling considered as unbreakable, even by successful businesswomen. I lost a few friends through it all, which saddened me. I understand what successful people mean when they say that once you've triumphed in what you achieved, some friends drop out of sight.

The Lioness, the Hunter

"There is no Wi-Fi in the forest, but I promise you will find a better connection."

– Anonymous

Lionesses hunt with other lionesses as a collective group, so I sought guidance from Dov Baron, my mentor. He taught me the importance of creating relationships with myself and with others. The big "aha" moment came when I acknowledged I was lost and disconnected from myself from the years of pretending I had it together. I was tired and exhausted from pretending that I had it together, that I didn't need emotional support, and that I didn't need assistance. I needed to love me for me – flaws and all. As a result, I gained greater strength and was empowered even more.

The first couple of years learning about the business were daunting and scary. I was averaging 14 hour days/six days per week. Days filled with hardship and the unknown future brought extreme stress and the health challenges of pre-menopause.

Some of the adversities I faced as a new businesswoman seemed funny a few years later. One late afternoon, the courier was delivering a shipment of kitchen gadgets, in the dark.

"You probably didn't pay your electricity bill," he laughed.

"Ha, ha," I laughed, sarcastically. No joke. The electrical company flipped off the switch as I failed to read the final reminder.

Another challenge was handling unhappy customers.

"I want a replacement right now for this piece of junk!" exclaimed the loud, angry voice of a disgruntled customer. I was brought to tears, too scared and shy to give voice.

Learning anything new has its ups and downs in the beginning. The days of experiencing mostly downs taught me the most about my inner strength. Like all of us, I needed that strength to carry on and not give up on ME. It was no longer like the swimming lessons, where I could easily throw in the towel and quit; I had too much invested in me and in the business.

Dov Baron instilled in me an important principle: "The *why* is always more important than the *how.*" Part of me knew how to operate my business as I had assistance from my brothers and my previous employer, Ron. They all offered wisdom and years of business expertise. I surrounded myself with those who have done better than I have.

My driving "why" is seeing me as worthy and having value. I became emotionally connected to knowing who Melanie is and who she can be. By making a new relationship with myself a priority in my life, I became an empowered woman of self-worth. When we embrace who we are and accept it as a package, we have greater self-esteem and confidence. When the driving "why" becomes our passion, we are no longer focused on the how; it naturally falls into place.

Without a doubt, the business had its challenges, ranging from adjusting to a decline in the economy, to ongoing staffing shortages. There were numerous occasions when I wanted to give up. Despite the family's emotional support and mentorship, I pushed through dark moments largely due to my self-discoveries experienced in Egypt. I reflected on how I mustered courage and strength to overcome my fears travelling solo for the first time. It would bring me back, from worrying and fretting, to a feeling of calmness. By weathering the emotional storm of Egypt, I would be calm and tranquil in the eye of any storm. This thought became a steppingstone of confidence in everything I did and was to go on to do. When you become strong and courageous after a lengthy, serious health challenge, or you have overcome a fear, you believe you can conquer anything.

Your fears are all self-imposed. Conquering them never comes by chance, but always occurs by choice.

Finding Your True Self and Calling

❝Life should not be a journey to the grave with the intention of arriving safely in a pretty and well preserved body, but rather to skid in broadside in a cloud of smoke, thoroughly used up, totally worn out, and loudly proclaiming "Wow! What a Ride!❞

— Hunter S. Thompson,
"The Proud Highway: Saga of a Desperate Southern Gentleman, 1955-1967"

WOW! What a ride! How many of us can say that? How many can claim they've lived life to the fullest … that we will slide in, used up and worn out? This is what I'd love to do!

I have dedicated this book to my mother. As I've said, she is the original 'gutsy lady'. She is a survivor, and has been all her life – from the time she was a little girl, escaping the Japanese invaders, to deciding to make a new life for herself in Canada. But I'll be honest with you, she was never able to live a joyous life. Maybe if she'd chosen a different path she would be, but even now, in her late 70s, she's not happy. What a tragedy to live life that way, but it is her choice.

Another friend of mine, Liz, understood the value of truly living – she packed more into her short 37 years than most people do in an 80 year lifetime.

At 36, she decided to quit her PR job in Los Angeles and go abroad and volunteer teaching English in Africa.

The poverty and lifestyle of those in Ghana was a shell shock for Liz and a world away from the glamorous life she led in LA.

But it quickly became apparent, within just days of her arrival, that this was Liz's passion. She adored giving back – loved the fact she was giving these children a chance to create a better future for themselves.

Liz stayed in Ghana until August of 2010. She had begun to feel ill and decided to head back to the U.S. for a few months. Upon arriving, she went to her doctor and explained her symptoms. When the test results came back, her world was thrown into turmoil.

"I am afraid I am the bearer of bad news," said Dr. Johnson. "You have stage four breast cancer."

Liz's life flashed before her eyes in that one second.

"I recommend we start chemotherapy straight away," he said.

And she did – the very next day.

Months of grueling treatments later, she was delivered a death sentence – the cancer had spread and there was nothing more that could be done to save her.

Liz had lived her life with no regrets and she was loved. She soaked in every single moment and experience that life had to offer, and I encourage you to do the same.

Live like there is no tomorrow. Someday you'll be right.

www.gutsyladytravel.com/www.gutsyladytravel.ca

Chapter Ten

Gutsy Lady Travel

❝Twenty years from now you will be more disappointed by the things you didn't do than by the ones you did do. So throw off the bowlines, sail away from the safe harbor. Catch the trade winds in your sails. Explore. Dream. Discover.❞

– Mark Twain

It requires courage to travel on your own for the first time and to live and experience the world.

We all know that there is always the first trailblazer full of zest and bravery, paving the way for the rest of us. These 'gutsy' ladies include Jeanne Baré. Jeanne was the first woman to circumnavigate the globe in 1766. She successfully masqueraded as a young man for the voyage.

Another adventurous lady was Nellie Bly, an American journalist who took a trip around the world in 72 days in 1888.

The gutsiest lady of all is my mother, who made a daring and valiant move from Guangdong, China to Victoria, BC at the young age of 21 to marry my father in an arranged marriage. I admire her strength and courage to move to a country on the other side of the globe, to marry a man based on a 'muscle man' photo. She spoke only Cantonese and knew nothing of the customs of Canadians or Canadian Chinese. Wouldn't you agree these are all brave women who inspire other women?

For some women, travelling solo isn't as simple as stepping on an airplane. It isn't always fun and games. Perhaps you yearn for a friend or partner to soak in the sights with. Maybe the thought of travelling on your own feels unsafe and leaves you feeling fearful. Think about it. Our amazing world isn't that big; we are one. In 2014, statistics indicated over 1.1 billion tourists travelled abroad. That's impressive, considering there were over 7.1 billion people on the planet in 2014. Europe ranked as the most visited region with 588 million visitors.[2] We rarely hear about serious attacks or harassment against women. We are smarter and wiser in our prime, so we possess good judgment. We have an inner GPS, our 'gut instinct'; we know whether a situation feels safe or not.

It was my unexpected solo trip in Egypt that demonstrated my conviction to assist women to travel courageously on their own. I was never that courageous lioness until I travelled to Egypt.

If travelling by yourself is not your full cup of tea, then there are other opportunities. You can mix it up by travelling solo and with a tour group. I had temporarily joined a local tour group to fill in the quiet gaps. For example, I joined a local five day tour of Croatia where I made new friends while visiting Plitvice Lakes National Park, a spectacular place that is best arranged with a tour. Another choice is to stay at places other than hotels where you can meet the locals and get to know them on a personal basis and see their authentic surroundings. I have stayed with kind and wonderful women who were strangers, in Cambodia and Hungary, but all that changed afterwards.

You will meet other solo female travellers. I often meet them at cafes, restaurants, and lineups at the museum. I had to wait four hours at the Zagreb train station in Croatia to make my way to Budapest. After an hour of taking interesting photos of doors and balconies, I was feeling bored and lonely. I was hankering to yap to another tourist. Unfortunately, since it was Sunday, no cafes or restaurants were open. The changing colours of the leaves and crisp air by mid-afternoon made it evident fall was beginning. I headed back to the small train station a third time, to pass time and to keep warm. This time, I saw a nicely dressed woman of similar age sitting on the wooden bench. We exchanged smiles.

"Hi. Where are you heading?" she asked, in a mountain southern accent.

"Hi. I'm Melanie. Hungary," I answered as I extended my hand to shake hers.

"Nice to meet you. I am Julie (Jules for short) from Nashville, Tennessee. I am heading to Austria," exclaimed Jules.

We immediately hit it off. By the time we boarded the train together, we were plotting our next rendezvous – Krakow, Poland. It would be happening in 10 short days. We chatted for hours as we passed time on the train.

To pass time, we commented on the various travellers sitting in the compartment. There was the 20-something blond youth with his heavy backpack, the couple in their 60s chatting in a foreign language, and a portly man dressed in a dark brown business suit discreetly glancing at the same magazine for over two hours.

"What do you think if I grab his magazine and hide it from him, before he gets back to his seat?" said Jules, with a mischievous look.

"Don't even think of touching that magazine!! You don't know what's on that magazine," I screamed in horror. We laughed until tears rolled down our cheeks when the pudgy, middle-aged, European man took his naughty magazine from his seat.

For three short, adventurous days, we cleared our lungs with deep breaths of salty air at the Wieliczka Salt Mines, made an adventurous local bus trip to Zakopane, and helped Jules shop for a real chinchilla fur hat. Though it was brief, the universe conspired to bring us together for a good time.

My unique and special journeys bring together a small, connected group of Boomer women to see more, do more, and be more; feeling more empowered. Whether you are travelling alone for the very first time or for the tenth time, the intimate groups provide guidance, safety nets, fun, adventures, and bonding with other like-minded women, and more importantly, laughter.

Lionesses often fail when they first learn to hunt, but that doesn't mean they never hunt again. In life, we all fall sometimes, but falling builds greater strength for our next adventure. No matter where you are, who you are, or where you are going, you were born as magnificent.

In my travel group, the lionesses travel together with prowess and each woman has her own skill set that contributes to a valued whole. There is strength and ability waiting to be developed within each of us. Together we laugh, connect, meditate, cry, confess fears, and have fun. My packages are designed to assist you to become the woman you were born to be.

How best to build unshakeable confidence? Consider travelling with me and living your own five star travel experience from a unique perspective. I mindfully design travel packages which are a combination of traditional trips and my own custom programs, and I actually travel with the groups.

In addition, each trip includes a private one-on-one coaching session along with pre-trip socializing events. I possess a wealth of travel experience, knowledge, and expertise with over 30 years' experience. I have travelled solo, travelled with individual women, and travelled with large groups. I also provide useful tips and tools for women to use in their travels.

All of the destinations are chosen for their beauty, travelling ease, and safety. No matter where you are, who you are, or where you are going, I provide 24/7 support. I am there to take you by the hand and support you on your own courageous journey. I will inspire you to do more. Wouldn't you agree there is something about travel experiences that captures your heart and soul, whether it is the joy of sharing an authentic Ramadan dinner with an Egyptian family, or practicing English with Cambodian monks?

It is time to take back your life and bring out your passport. So why not? There is nothing holding you back except the baggage you carry within you. Let's set that aside, travel light, and live fully.

Learn to laugh at the irony, the danger, and the quirks in your life.
Travel can reveal all of these and more.

www.gutsyladytravel.com/www.gutsyladytravel.ca

Conclusion

Do You Have the Courage to Travel?

❝Travel brings power and love back into your life.❞

– Rumi

It's time to explore this wonderful world and stop putting your dreams on hold – embrace that thirst for adventure with gusto. Be willing to dive into the assorted chocolates and savour each bite.

I have shared my stories and others, but I left a very special one for last that will truly leave you inspired.

Carol is a friend that I got to know for a short period of time. She was adventurous, 72-years-young, full of a zest for life, full of spirit, and very passionate about travel. Last year, we spent three fun days in Rome, Italy between our solo trips. She also met Bob, a handsome young 50-year-old man, upon her arrival.

"Sorry I didn't call you last night, Melanie, but I had a slight diversion. I met Bob near my hotel and he invited me out for a drink," she explained.

"Wow! You haven't even set foot in Italy for 24 hours and you have already met an Italian. Ooh la-la," I laughed.

"Well, he's actually Canadian. Let's meet for lunch at the piazza at one o'clock and I'll give you the dirt."

We spent a delightful afternoon lunching at the café as we shared our solo travel experiences. Later, we visited the Capuchin Crypt. Carol loves anything morbid and is a big fan of horror movies. I am the opposite, but this crypt fascinated me with the three-dimensional wallpaper, consisting of the bones of 4,000 Capuchin monks.

"Ok. You see the old security guard at the end of the hall?" whispered Carol, as her eyes glanced to the right.

"Yep! His eyes are fixed on us," I waved my arms at him with a cute smile and a wink.

"Stop that! We don't need any further attention. Try to distract him so I can snap a couple of photos of these skulls."

"Okay, but make it snappy." We both chuckled.

It wasn't long before we heard, "YOU! No photo!" He shouted as his finger pointed directly at us. We were giggling like little girls as we walked past him.

For the next two days, Carol was two-timing. Perfectly orchestrating her time between Bob and me. She and Bob strolled along picturesque Villa Borghese Park, and later, enjoyed a candlelight dinner. With me, she squeezed in a Caravaggio experience, explored the Pantheon, and lunched at Vittorio Emmanuel II Monument.

"You're amazing, girl! You have more energy than I do. I am so happy we met in Rome. I had a great time with you. It was worth meeting up for three days!"

"I am really happy we met, despite this cold I have," she exclaimed. We were going our separate ways – Cinque Terre tour for Carol and for me, Budapest, to visit my friend Ani.

She returned home in late October, still with a nasty cold. I urged her to see the doctor and she did.

"I can't believe you went to see the doctor and all you chatted about was his and your summer trips to Italy," I said, shaking my head. After pressing the matter a second time, she went back to see her doctor. She told me her news.

"Melanie, I have bone cancer," she said somberly.

"I am sad to hear that," I replied with disbelief. I hugged her with tears in my eyes.

My heart sank. I was completely lost for words. It was difficult for me to accept her condition. I thought she had a bad flu bug. Six months later, I went to visit her in hospice.

"Carol, you know I am writing a book to inspire women to travel and to teach them how they can build unshakeable confidence by travelling. As an expert solo traveller, what would you say to those women who haven't travelled solo or haven't travelled before?" I asked.

"I want you to tell as many women as you can, to travel as much as they can, regardless of their age. See the world! Yeah, they'll be scared at first, but after that, they'll be fearless. You and I know that. And if they are afraid to travel alone, they would be smart to travel with you. I lived my life fully, and I am happy that I got to experience what the world has to offer," she proudly announced as tears filled her eyes.

Carol transitioned 10 days later.

She was a remarkable woman who lived every single day with zest. I encourage you to take a leaf from her book and do the same.

You can be a passenger or you can lead in life – the decision is up to you. My adventures, like yours, are just beginning. Any journey can be priceless and your experiences, when faced boldly, will forever change your life.

If you would like to learn more about yourself, travel, and to unleash the courage already within you, drop me a line and let's have a conversation.

Visit www.gutsyladytravel.com and contact me at +1 604 222 7811 or info@gutsyladytravel.com.

Live like you've never lived before!

---

www.gutsyladytravel.com/www.gutsyladytravel.ca

Here's a gift for you.
In under 3 minutes, you'll discover...

- How to travel solo in a heartbeat

- The #1 thing that is causing you to lose sleep!

- The secret to becoming a more content and confident woman

    And much, MUCH More...

Download COMPLIMENTARY guide at:

http://www.gutsyladytravel.com/report

References

[1] Glendenning, Barry. (2012, January 25) 50 stunning Olympic moments No 11: Eric Moussambani flails way to glory. *The Guardian*

[2] (2015, January 27) Over 1.1 billion tourists travelled abroad in 2014. UNWTO *(United Nations World Tourism Organization)* Retrieved from: http://media.unwto.org/press-release/2015-01-27/over-11-billion-tourists-travelled-abroad-2014

Baron, Dov, Founder, www.fullmontyleadership.com. Named by *Inc Magazine* as one of the Top 100 Great Leadership Speakers to hire.

http://www.en.wikipedia.org/ - Wikipedia

http://www.pinterest.com – Pinterest

http://www.goodreads.com - Goodreads

Made in the USA
San Bernardino, CA
13 March 2016